So You Want to Become a Flight Attendant?

Copyright © 2016 by Amerika Young
www.Freedomlifeexperience.com

Published by Freedom Life Experience
Cover Design by Amerika Young

ISBN 978-0-692-76260-8

All rights reserved. No part of this work may be reproduced, distributed, or transmitted in any form or by any means without the prior written permission of the publisher.

TABLE OF CONTENTS

5	WELCOME
8	HISTORY OF THE FLIGHT ATTENDANT
10	REQUIREMENTS
15	WORKING AS A FLIGHT ATTENDANT
32	PACK YOUR BAGS!
36	STAY SAFE, PROTECT YOURSELF!
39	LET'S GET PAID!
42	BENEFITS
45	RESERVE FLIGHT ATTENDANT
52	LINE HOLDER FLIGHT ATTENDANT
54	PERSONAL LIFE
58	LET'S SET UP YOUR RESUME!
64	HOW TO DRESS FOR THE INTERVIEW
69	BODY LANGUAGE
71	INTERVIEWS
80	NOW WHAT? PREPARE FOR TRAINING!
85	AIRPORT CODES
87	24-HOUR CLOCK
88	KEY TERMS

FIND YOUR PLACE IN THE SKIES

"You can find a spot in aviation if you look, if you want. A place in your dreams. Aviation is 100 years old and it's brand new. You can help take it into the future. Freedom, responsibility, they're not just words. Join us!"

-Harrison Ford

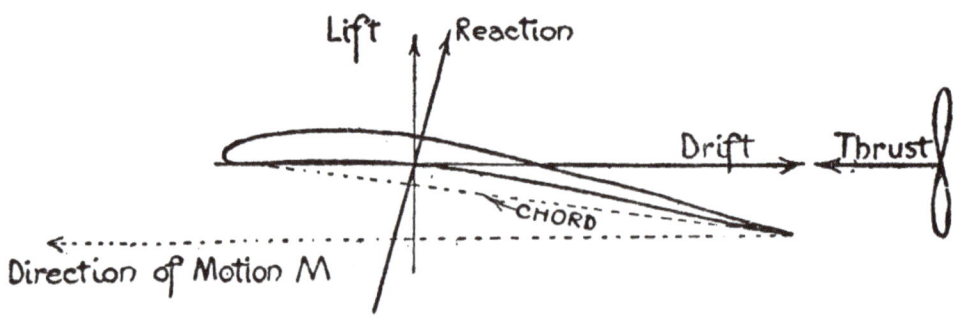

WELCOME

Dear Future Flight Attendant,

I hope you are ready for the flight of your life! Being a flight attendant brings bundles of amazing opportunities and experiences. You will have a lifetime of stories to tell. By the same token, be patient with the process. It can take anywhere from a few weeks to a few months to take off on your first flight. If you don't hear back right away after you've applied, don't become discouraged! Some airlines will take two to three months to even ask for an interview. Believe me, the wait is worth it! Take the time to go through this handbook, dig deep into your soul, and answer all of the questions completely. I will share the ins and outs and even some top-level classified secrets to becoming a flight attendant. If you have any questions throughout this handbook, or during your future travels, do not hesitate to contact me! I will be here for you every step (and flight) along the way.

Cheers,
Amerika

I TRADED MY CUBE FOR A TUBE!

I went to college, got a 9-5 job, and thought that was the career path I was going to stay on… forever. I powered through that mundane routine for five years and then realized that being stuck in a cube day-in and day-out was *not* the life for me. I felt like I was having a quarter(ish) life crisis and I needed a change in my career - a change in my life. With some encouragement from family and friends, I made the leap and applied to be a flight attendant. It was the absolute *best* decision of my life. I turned in my two weeks' notice and I traded my cube for a tube! An airplane, that is! I don't mind the idea of having stable roots, but I have an absolute addiction for wings. I am forever looking to the sky.

"A mile of highway will take you a mile. A mile of runway will take you anywhere!"
-Anonymous

SPREAD YOUR WINGS

As you embark on this adventure, you must remember to be confident! So many others *dream* of being a flight attendant, but YOU are the one who has the courage to apply and shoot for the sky with this incredible career. Being a flight attendant isn't just a career, it's a lifestyle. There will be ups and downs (and turbulence along the way) but remember, hold your head up high, look forward, and keep your arms and legs inside the aisles at all times!

Does the thought of clicking the "submit" button on your application sound scary? As the saying goes, "If your dreams don't scare you, they aren't big enough!" Are you tired of every day being the same? Are you tired of punching a time clock and doing work that feels meaningless to you? Are the kids all grown up and out of the house and you're ready for an adventure of your own? Apply to be a flight attendant! The journey is liberating. Being a flight attendant does take a special kind of character, but since you have purchased this handbook and are taking the time to complete the questions, I believe you have that special kind of character. They say the sky is the limit, but you will break even that barrier because you will be working at 35,000 feet. Who else gets to do that? (Other than pilots of course!)

FIRST FLIGHT

December 17, 1903

The Wright Brothers took the first flight Kitty Hawk, NC

"For once you have tasted flight you will walk the earth with your eyes
turned skywards, or there you have been and there you will long to return." **-Leonardo da Vinci**

HISTORY OF THE FLIGHT ATTENDANT

For centuries the human race has been curious about the concept of flying. On December 17th 1903, the Wright Brothers made the first successful flight - and in the hundred years following, aviation has made huge leaps and bounds. The original word for flight attendant was "steward". It derives from the time of ship transportation when the Chief Steward was the lead crew member who directed operations, planned menus, and often cooked on the ship. Accordingly, airlines adopted the term *steward* and *stewardess*.

In 1912, Heinrich Kubis became the world's first steward. At first only men were allowed to be stewards, but in 1930, United Airlines hired 25-year-old registered nurse Ellen Church as the first female flight attendant. Other airlines quickly followed suit and began to hire registered nurses as stewardesses or "air hostesses". For many years it was mandatory to be a nurse in order to become a flight attendant. However, during World War II the requirement to be a nurse was lifted because so many nurses were enlisted in the war.

Soon it became customary that only females were allowed to be flight attendants. There were strict physical requirements that each applicant had to meet. They had to be "petite", weigh between 100-118 pounds, be between 20-26 years of age, single, and they had to go through physical inspections several times a year. They were fired immediately if they didn't meet the physical requirements, got married, or became pregnant.

In 1968 the age restriction was lifted and in 1971 flight attendants were no longer required to be female - males were finally allowed to apply. By the 1980's the no-marriage rule was lifted and by the 1990's, the weight and appearance restrictions were relaxed as well.

THE FIRST FLIGHT ATTENDANTS WERE REQUIRED TO BE REGISTERED NURSES

IN 1971, MEN WERE ALLOWED TO APPLY TO BE FLIGHT ATTENDANTS

UNTIL 1968, FLIGHT ATTENDANTS WERE FIRED IF THEY CHOSE TO GET MARRIED

AGE

Across various airlines, the minimum age requirement ranges from 18 to 21 - there is no maximum age. So don't think for a second that you are too old to apply or that it's too late to start a new adventure! No matter what age or stage you are at in life, it's never too late to taste flight and chase your dreams in the clouds. Believe in yourself! You are never too old to start a new endeavor!

"Age is an issue of mind over matter. If you don't mind, it doesn't matter."
–Mark Twain

EDUCATION

Do I need to take classes or go to school to be a flight attendant?
The answer to that question is no! You can find "flight attendant schools" out there, but they are not a requirement or truly necessary. The airline that hires you will send you to their own training school which will last anywhere from four to eight weeks. Training is very specific to each airline and their material cannot be purchased anywhere. (Heads up - some airlines might not pay you while you are in training, but there won't be any out-of-pocket training expenses expected of you either.)

Do I need a college degree to be a flight attendant?
Each airline is a little different, but most of them do not require a four-year degree. Some airlines might like to see that you have some college education, but it is not a must. However, a high school diploma or GED is required for all applicants. There are a multitude of flight attendants out there who actually have a lot of education. I've seen everything from lawyers to engineers to teachers who changed lifestyles to become flight attendants. And why not, it's the best job ever!

EXPERIENCE

Most often times, no previous experience as a flight attendant is necessary. Do you have any experience in the customer service field? Great! That will be something we will highlight in your resume later on in this handbook. If you don't have any customer service experience, don't fret. There will be other ways to showcase how you've delivered service in the past or that your character is perfect for the job. A lot of flight attendants are hired straight out of college and this is their first "real" job.

HEIGHT

The general height requirement is between 5'0" and 6'3". Check with the airline(s) you are applying for. Some may not require a specified height, but will test your "reach range". This is because each style of airplane has different ceiling heights. Regional airlines have smaller airplanes and mainline airlines have bigger, taller airplanes.

WEIGHT

In the United States, airlines may not discriminate based on weight, but they *can* specify that your weight should be within decent proportion to your height. You may be required to strap into a jump seat. If you fit in the straps, then you meet the weight requirements.

VISION

Your vision must be clear enough to perform everyday duties. Corrective lenses or glasses are permitted.

> "OF ALL THE BOOKS IN THE WORLD, THE BEST STORIES ARE FOUND BETWEEN THE PAGES OF A PASSPORT"
> *-ANONYMOUS*

PASSPORT

You must have a valid passport at the time of hire from the country of which you are a citizen. If you do not have a passport or it is expired, it could take up to sixteen weeks to receive. Your passport needs to be valid for at least three months beyond the date of your interview.

TIP! If you live in or near a passport agency, it is possible to make an appointment and they can issue you your passport in as little as two weeks. It is necessary to set up an appointment with these offices. Passports are generally good for ten years. If your passport is due to expire shortly, take the action needed to have it renewed. Airlines won't let you fly with an expired passport. Period. Even if your trip is domestic, be sure to keep your passport with you just in case the airline needs to divert you or change your route in the middle of the trip.

IDENTIFICATION

You will need a government-issued identification, whether that is a state photo ID or driver's license.

BIRTH CERTIFICATE

You will need to provide your birth certificate at either the end of the interview or upon hire when you fill out paperwork.

SCREENING

Background Check

Airlines will conduct a thorough background check. You must pass this to continue forward in the hiring process.

Finger Printing

Security is incredibly strict when working for or dealing with an airline. You will be finger printed however, nowadays they have digital finger printing instead of old fashioned ink and paper. It's much less messy!

Drug Testing

Drug tests are mandatory and you will be provided with directions on where and when the drug testing needs to take place. Drink lots of water the day of your test. You don't want to have to return at a later date to take the test again if you can't produce enough for your sample.

LANGUAGE

Check with your airline to see what their language requirements are. Any airline based in the U.S will require you to be able to read, speak, and understand English. Some airlines may be looking for bilingual skills or offer translator positions.

Translator Programs

Can you read, speak, and understand a second language? If your airline flies to a destination where your second language is spoken, they may require at least one flight attendant on board that speaks the language of that destination. There may be additional compensation for this kind of support. You could be in high demand! There will be a test or an interview to ensure that you can efficiently communicate in that language.

CITIZENSHIP

If you are working in the United States, being a citizen may not be a requirement. If you are not a citizen, then you will have to provide proof that you are eligible to work in the U.S. You will always need to carry your passport with you when you work. If you are applying to an airline out of the United States, check for their visa or citizenship requirements.

WORKING AS A FLIGHT ATTENDANT

BASES
Bases are the airports which airlines mainly operate out of. They are generally located in major cities such as Denver, New York and Seattle. All trips that you work will originate out of your home base. For example; If you are based in Miami, FL. Every trip you are assigned starts with a flight out of Miami and on the last day of the trip the last flight will end in Miami.

RELOCATING
While working from of your home base is required, you do not always have to live in your home base area. If you are on reserve (see page 45) then you will be required to live in your base city for the duration of the days that you are on-call. Airlines will most likely not pay for you to relocate. They will often give you three to five days between training and your first day of work to find a new place to live and move to your home base. It's not a lot of time, but knowing this in advance will help you make a plan of how you are going to relocate. If you are planning on relocating, I would suggest renting a "crash pad" for a month or a few weeks until you get a better idea of the city you will be living in. If you are on reserve, scheduling may only give you 90 minutes up to two hours' notice to make it to the airplane for the trip. Consider living as close to the airport as possible.

COMMUTING BETWEEN YOUR HOME AND BASE

A large percentage of flight crews do not live in their home base city, but they commute, whether that is driving or flying. If your airline allows you to travel for free, then it may be possible for you to live in a different city and commute to work. However, when considering commuting, remember that you may have to fly into base a day early and get a hotel for the night if you have an early departure the next morning, or if you know flights are tight and there's a chance you won't make it to work the day of.

Commuting is said to take *years* off a person's life. It can be very stressful trying to make it to work on time or running across the airport at the end of your trip hoping to make the last flight home of the night. Is it possible to do this? Yes. Just be prepared and know what you are getting into. Some airlines have a two-flight policy where you must show that you have listed for and missed two flights into your home base due to no space available before calling off your trip. Once you've proven that you've given yourself the required amount of opportunities to make it, they will dismiss your trip and make note on your record of a "no commute". It is possible to get in trouble if you have too many "no commutes" on your record. See your airline for their commuting policy.

YOU CAN LIVE ANYWHERE IN THE COUNTRY

CRASH PADS

Crash pads are either an apartment or a house shared by multiple flight attendants who do not live in their base city but need a place to sleep before or after their trip or while on reserve or commute to work. Depending on the city, crash pads come fully furnished and can run between $300-$400 a month just for the use of a bed and the utilities inside. Many people who commute and often have early flights out in the morning will rent a bed in a crash pad and fly in the night before and stay there. Be prepared for multiple beds or even bunk beds in each room. Crash pads are often shared with upwards of 10-20 other people, but keep in mind that everyone has different times and days they will be there, so the chances of everyone being at the crash pad at one time is rare. Remember, you're using the crash pad basically just to sleep or kill time before your next flight. Most crash pads will allow you to pay month-to-month rather than make you sign a lease.

Let's say you are on reserve or you commute between home and your base. You might want to consider going in with a couple other people and splitting an apartment lease. This way you can have your own space, your own room, and only share common areas such as the bathrooms and kitchen. Depending on the cost of living, you may be able to split a nicer apartment for the same cost as a crash pad.

> "I'D RISK THE FALL.
> JUST TO KNOW HOW IT FEELS TO FLY."
> –ANONYMOUS

TRANSPORTATION

If you're based in a major city such as New York City or Philadelphia there may be convenient mass transportation and you can reside there without having a car. If you're based in another city that does not have a mass transportation system, you will need to have a reliable car. Few crash pads will actually have the use of a shared car.

SENIORITY

Everything in the airlines is based on seniority. How you bid for flights, how you're awarded schedules, how you bid for vacation, how you get a seat on the airplane, when you fly as a passenger (which we call a non-revenue passenger or non-rev). For each person that retires or quits, that puts you one spot higher on the seniority list. Each time another person is hired, that puts you further from the bottom of the food chain. Hurry up and apply now because airlines are hiring like crazy! The sooner you get hired, the higher your seniority will be!

FLIGHT ATTENDANT UNION

Many airlines have flight attendant unions. A union is a group of workers who have come together to form an organization that represents all workers and protects them against unfair rules set forth by a company for its members. A union has a goal of setting safety standards and achieving higher pay and benefits such as retirement, medical, and other compensation. If your company has a union, every flight attendant pays monthly dues to their union. Should you refuse to be a part of the flight attendant union, there is often a monthly fee charged regardless. If you get in trouble at work, immediately arrange for a union representative to meet with you and your supervisor to negotiate during the meeting. Having someone from the union with you may help lessen the severity of your punishment or keep it from getting worse. Some airlines do not have unions. There can be pros and cons to this however, an airline without a union may dismiss you for any reason they'd like at any time should you get in trouble.

DAYS IN A ROW

NO MORE THAN 6 DAYS IN A ROW

24 HOUR REST PERIOD EVERY 6 DAYS

NO MORE THAN 35 HOURS IN 7 DAYS

Depending on your contract with your airline, you most likely cannot work more than six days in a row without a 24-hour rest period between flights. Nor are you allowed to work more than 35 hours within a seven-day period.

When you become a line holder, it will be up to you to make sure you do not exceed the rules that are set up by the Federal Aviation Administration and your union. Your airline may not always be able to catch or monitor how many days in a row you've worked. You and the airline can get in trouble if the days and hours are exceeded. Go back to those elementary school rules and keep a planner with you!

Many airlines have checks and balances in place to catch errors, but it's ultimately <u>your</u> responsibility. If you are on reserve, scheduling may try to push the envelope when they are tight and in need of flight coverage immediately. Know your contract or your flight rules and don't be afraid to speak up if they are breaking these rules.

I was once assigned a trip that would have put me outside of the rules set forth by my union contract. Because I was educated on these rules, I was able to turn down the trip without getting in trouble. I was dismissed from the trip once scheduling realized their mistake.

GETTING THROUGH SECURITY

NORMAL SECURITY LINE

When traveling in uniform, most airports have an employee line, allowing you to bypass the long line and proceed directly to a TSA agent for processing. You are not held to the same standards for liquids in your bags such as soap and shampoo but you are held to the same standards as far as sharp objects or weapons which are never allowed.

A fellow flight attendant and friend of mine was stopped in security for having a metal butter knife in her bag. She had to give it up immediately. No more butter for her bread!

If you are traveling out of uniform, you must abide by all federal regulations for travel and security; your liquids must be under three ounces and fit in a quart size bag.

KNOWN CREW MEMBER

This is one of the best inventions and benefits in my life! Not all airports in the US have Known Crew Member (KCM) security operations but a growing amount are coming to airports. There is an additional application and background check to go through to be cleared for KCM. You will receive a card with a barcode to scan at the time you enter the security checkpoint. Scan your barcode at the desk, present your crew member badge, and an additional form of government issued ID such as a driver's license or passport. Your photo and identification will pop up on the TSA agent's screen with a confirmation if you are cleared. They will quickly check your badge and ID, then send you on your merry way!

> **KNOWN CREW MEMBER IS THE BEST THING SINCE SLICED BREAD!**
> (With or without butter)

As of 2015, you are no longer required to be in uniform to go through Known Crew Member. That is a wonderful thing when you are traveling for personal pleasure!

When you are traveling for personal pleasure and don't wish to wear your uniform, check with all airports you are traveling to if they have Known Crew Member. Once, I didn't check and just assumed an airport had the option. When I got there I realized they didn't offer the service and I did not have a uniform with me. I had to remove all my liquids and put them into my now checked bag, which of course I wasn't originally planning on checking. When I went through "normal" security I was immediately stopped and my bags were searched. I don't know about you, but nothing is worse than a complete stranger tearing out my underwear and throwing the contents of my bag across a table in front of everyone in security. I was mortified and the agent wouldn't tell me what he was looking for. At the very bottom of my bag was my favorite perfume and the bottle exceeded the three-ounce limit. It was too late to go back and put the perfume in my checked bag. After confiscating my perfume, the guy stood back and said "Do you want to repack it or do you want me too?" I was red hot in the face and insisted I would do it.

By applying for this service, you are promising to adhere to strict regulations and to honor the no-weapons policy. You are still subject to search at any time going through KCM. Don't abuse it. It truly is a privilege.

PASSENGER BAGGAGE

| BAGGAGE FEES ARE AT AN ALL TIME HIGH AND RISING |  | CARRY-ON BAGGAGE IS ALSO ON THE RISE | | THIS CAUSES MORE FLIGHT ATTENDANT INJURIES DUE TO LIFTING BAGS |

With airlines charging more and more every year for passengers to check their bags, more people are packing everything they can in their carry-on bag and taking it onto the airplane with them. This can make for some very heavy bags. I lift my own suitcase into the overhead bin every day and I can tell you it's a handful to get into up there! Lifting one bag a day, your own bag, is no big deal, but I guarantee you on almost every single flight you work, there will be someone asking you for help with lifting their bag. They are going to give you every reason under the stars why they can't lift it. "I just had back surgery." "My shoulder is bad." "I can't lift anything over 5 pounds."

I once had a shorter lady look at a flight attendant who was even shorter than she was and told her she needed the flight attendant to lift her bag for her because she was too short. The flight attendant looked the passenger dead in the eye and said, "I'm shorter than you are and I can get my bag in the overhead bin." Then she walked away.

**YOU PACK IT, YOU STACK IT
YOU BRING IT, YOU SLING IT
YOU TOW IT, YOU STOW IT
I TOUCH IT, I TAG IT**

I cannot stress to you enough how important it is **NOT** to volunteer to help passengers lift their luggage into the overhead bins. It is not a natural motion to lift things over your head and luggage can get very heavy. I have seen many people get injured trying to lift a passenger's bag. Then they are out of work for weeks or months due to the injury and possibly even need surgery. There are a few things you can do or say in order not to sound rude or unhelpful. If someone asks me to help lift their luggage, I will say one of two things.

"If your bag is too heavy for you to lift, I would be more than happy to check it for free to your final destination." Then I would tag the bag and have it sent under the airplane to the luggage compartment. Check to see if your airline offers complimentary bag check at the gate. It makes everyone's life easier on the airplane and at the gate.

or...

"If you can lift it up, I will guide your bag into the overhead bin." This way you are helping them, but you aren't doing any heavy lifting.

I have found that many times a kind passenger will stand up and help a fellow passenger who is struggling with their bag. I once had a passenger ask why I offered to check someone else's bag but wouldn't lift it. I politely explained that if I had lifted that passenger's bag into the overhead bin, then I would have to help everyone else and I see 175 passengers three times a day. They quickly understood why.

HOTELS YOUR HOME AWAY FROM HOME

STAYING AT HOTELS

Hotels will quickly become your home away from home. The airline will book and pay for your hotel accommodations. Hotel locations, phone numbers, and transportation information should be provided to you for each night at the beginning of your trip. Your stay could be anywhere from 11 to 32 hours depending on the flights of your trip.

It's important to remain safety-conscious while on your layover. Do not tell passengers what hotel you'll be staying at. Politely decline their request. When you get to your room, check behind doors, in closets, behind curtains, under the bed and in the bathroom. I had an experience where a hotel double-booked my room and when I got there someone was already occupying it. As I opened the door I scared the "living daylights" out of the guy. That is why you check your room first.

When your room is clear, shut and lock the door using both the deadbolt and the chain or door hook for extra safety. That top hook will stop the door from being opened more than an inch or two should someone be able to open the door or accidentally have a duplicate key to your room. Should someone attempt to get in, call the hotel front desk immediately.

SLAM-CLICKER:
A FLIGHT ATTENDANT WHO SLAMS THE DOOR, CLICKS THE LOCK & DOESN'T COME OUT UNTIL THE END OF TIME.
ZZZZZ....

SLAM-CLICKER

SLEEP TIGHT. DON'T LET THE BED BUGS BITE.

OKAY, BUT SERIOUSLY... Before you get all settled into your room, check your bed or beds for bed bugs. At the top of the bed, pull back the sheets including any mattress covers and check for bugs. Bed bugs tend to hide out at the top edge of the bed. You will be able to see them if they are present.

If you don't see anything, then you are good to go and you can put the sheets back. If you do find something, report it to the hotel front desk immediately and contact the airline immediately as well. Your airline should have a department to handle these kinds of things, especially if you have a union.

When you are leaving your hotel room, have everything packed up and by the door. Then do a final walk through of the room. Check under the sheets, on the sides of the bed, behind the bathroom door and in the shower. Check for phone chargers. Bring the room key with you just in case you forget something after you've left the room. You may not have time to get a new key from the desk and return in time for the van.

PICK A KEY CARD, ANY KEY CARD!!

I once couldn't figure out why my room key was not working. I tried it multiple times out of frustration. I took one more look at my key card and realized that it was the one from the hotel the night before. Soon, you'll have a whole collection of cards!

HERE IS AN ACRONYM TO HELP YOU FIGURE OUT IF YOU ARE HEALTHY AND FIT FOR DUTY

ILLNESS
Are you suffering from any illness or symptom that will affect your job performance?

MEDICATION
Are you taking any drugs, whether prescription or over the counter? Will this medication affect your job performance?

STRESS
Are you worried about other factors in your life? Stress, whether caused by work conditions or outside situations, can cause you to become distracted from the task at hand and reduce job performance and decision making.

ALCOHOL
Alcohol should not be consumed within 8 hours before your flight. Some airlines have a policy of 12 hours. Blood alcohol level should not be above .04%.

FATIGUE
Have you had enough sleep? When you are fatigued, it can lessen your ability to make smart and quick decisions. It raises your chances of making mistakes, sometimes costly. Check with your airline's policy about calling off a trip due to fatigue.

EATING
Have you had enough to eat? Eating fuels the brain just as much as it fuels the rest of the body. Nobody likes to be "hangry"

STAYING HEALTHY

One of the biggest challenges of working as a flight attendant can be staying healthy and eating well. When you're on the go for several days in a row, it can be really easy to grab a cheeseburger and French fries with a giant coke each day or snack on the leftover airplane snacks. Remember that uniform you bought when you first started working? You don't want to outgrow them! Airport cheeseburgers on occasion won't cause you to swell up overnight, but it can add up quickly.

If you are trying to stay healthy, save money and bring your own food. However, it can be very difficult to keep your food cold on a long trip. One of the best purchases you can make will be a good lunch bag. I didn't care for the lunch bag my airlines suggested. I wasn't required to purchase it, so I did my research and found one that I like better. Now that you have a good lunch bag, try to pack healthy snacks and meals as much as possible.

YOUR WAISTLINE & YOUR WALLET WILL
THANK YOU FOR PACKING FOOD FOR EACH TRIP.

DON'T DO THIS →

KEEPING FOOD CHILLED

You'll need something to keep your food chilled on-the-go. Look for the little medical ice bags that are often found in the pharmacy section of your local store. They will have a screw-on lid you can fill with ice and close them up tight. They are made so they don't sweat as the ice melts. Fill up the bag as often as you need. You can get ice from the airplane or hotels.

Some hotel rooms come standard with small refrigerator units. Other hotels you'll have to ask if they can have one delivered to your room. If they say they charge for refrigerator rentals, ask if they waive the fee for crew members or offer a discount.

> **-WARNING-**
> DO NOT PUT FOOD ON THE TOP SHELF OR NEAR THE FREEZER SECTION OF THE HOTEL ROOM REFRIGERATOR. YOU'LL WAKE UP TO FOOD POPSICLES.

HEATING FOOD

On your layovers you will stay at an array of different hotels. Not all hotels are created equal. Some hotels will provide a mini fridge and a microwave while others provide nothing but a bucket for you to put ice in. Sometimes after you get off the airplane all you want is a hot meal. Well, when there is not a microwave in the room that can be very difficult. One of the best things I carry in my bag is a portable hot plate. It looks like a little insulated lunch bag with a hot plate inside. I plug it in and put my food inside and by the time I have settled into my room and taken a shower I have a hot meal waiting for me.

HEALTH AND FITNESS

Staying fit while you are on the go can be tough, but it CAN be done! Be sure to pack your tennis shoes and workout clothes for each trip. Most hotels will have a fitness room. Some hotels will have a tiny room the size of a postage stamp with a handful of dumbbells and a broken treadmill and call it a "gym" while other hotels will have a full-on fitness facility complete with every type of weight machine and cardio equipment you can imagine. Most hotels are somewhere in between. If the hotel doesn't have a good gym and it's nice out, go for a walk or a run if you're in a nice area. It would be smart to plan out where you are going first. For safety, either take another crew member with you or tell someone where you are going and how to get ahold of you. Do whatever you can to stay healthy and in shape. Get creative!

CALLING OUT SICK

#1 DAY FLIGHT ATTENDANTS CALL OUT SICK: HALLOWEEN

During training, it was instilled in me to fear scheduling and their calls. I felt like my world would come to an end if I didn't answer the phone on time or if I didn't make it to the airport on time. About a year into flying, I got so sick that I could hardly stand up. I was terrified to call out sick because I didn't want to get in trouble, but I was still on reserve so I was hoping I could ride out the next few days and not get called out. So of course, I got a call from scheduling for a two-day trip. I got up to pack my bags, but my roommates convinced me that I was being unreasonable and should not work when I was that ill nor subject 175 other passengers and coworkers to what I had contracted. I called scheduling back and told them I needed to be removed from my trip due to being sick. I got an earful from the scheduler about how I needed to call out sick before I got called out to work a trip. You only get so many sick calls a year before you need a doctor's note or have a meeting with your supervisor. Be smart, use those sick calls when you need them. Nothing is worse than working on an airplane while you are sick. Symptoms at 30,000 feet become *far* worse. You also run the risk of damaging or blowing out an ear drum if you have a head cold. The recovery time can be weeks to months. Your doctor will not allow you to fly if you have a damaged ear drum. No flying equals no paycheck.

This story isn't meant to scare you but to show you how important it is to put your health first. Your life and your health are far more important than finishing a trip. Check with your airline, but many companies will allow you to call out sick for up to 21 days in a row and have it count as one sick occurrence. My company allows four sick occurrences per year with each occurrence up to 21 days long.

IT'S TIME TO LOOK LIKE A FABULOUS FLIGHT ATTENDANT!

UNIFORMS

Each airline has its own style of uniforms and you will be required to purchase your own uniforms. Beware that many companies will require you to purchase a minimum dollar amount. I had to purchase a minimum of $700 in clothing, but it was put on an account and a payment was withdrawn from my paycheck each month until the uniforms were paid off. I have to say, it's quite fun to dress for the part!

CONSIDER ALL THE POSSIBILITIES

When picking out pieces for your uniform, be sure to diversify. Think about the types of clothes that will suit you and what you think you will wear. I made the mistake of buying five pairs of pants and only one dress. Turns out I can't stand the pants and I love the dress. I couldn't return the pants because they came pre-hemmed, so I had to buy an additional dress at an additional cost. Possible options include:

- Short Sleeve Shirts
- Long Sleeve Shirts
- Button-Up Shirts
- Knit Shirts
- Vests
- Slacks or Pants
- Heavy Sweaters
- Light Sweater
- Dresses
- Skirts
- Winter Coat
- Dress Coat
- Ties
- Bow Ties
- Belts
- Scarves

GETTING YOUR WINGS

As soon as you complete your training, you will be given your wings and you'll be ready to fly! Each crew member, both pilots and flight attendants, wears a set of wings over their heart on their uniforms. Wear them with pride!

PACK YOUR BAGS!

Flight Attendant be like...

You will learn to pack your entire universe into just two bags. One larger rolling carry-on size bag and a smaller tote. When I pack for a trip, I pack clothes, shoes, toiletries and anything I don't need within arm's length in my larger bag. Very few airlines may require crew to check their bags on each trip. In my smaller tote, I carry everything that I could possibly need on the plane. I include required items provided by the airline plus an array of personal items.

HERE'S A GREAT LIST OF ITEMS TO CHOOSE FROM WHEN PACKING YOUR FLIGHT ATTENDANT BAG

- Breath mints
- Floss poppers
- Eye drops
- Lotion
- Snack
- Phone charger
- Reading glasses
- Contact solution
- Contact case
- Lip gloss/Chapstick
- Benadryl
- External battery
- Vitamin C
- Tea
- Ice bag
- Hot plate
- Cough drops
- Hand sanitizer
- Headphones
- Pen
- Notebook
- Flashlight
- Soda can opener
- Hot water bag
- Benadryl
- Earplugs
- Eye mask
- Advil
- Hair ties and bobby pins
- Comfortable shoes
- Oven mitt or oven glove
- Cough drops
- Gum

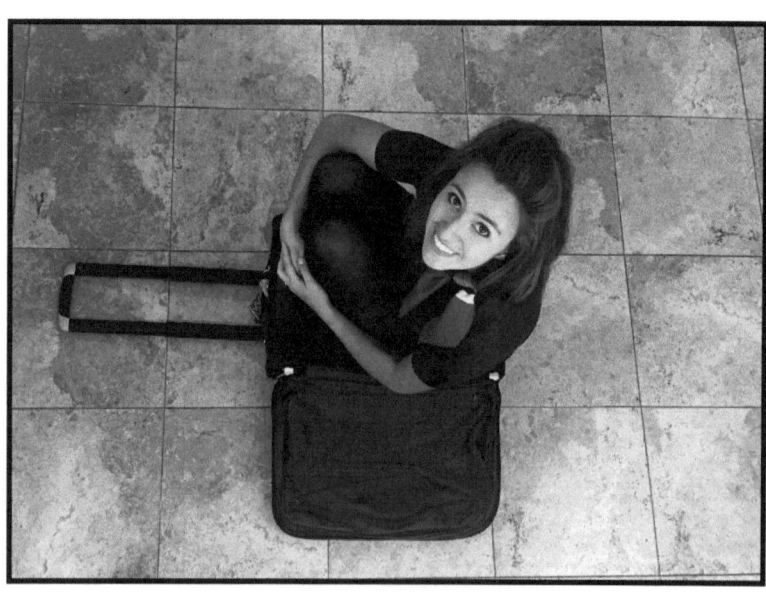

MARK YOUR TERRITORY!

NO, NOT LIKE THAT!

Have you noticed when you travel that a majority of the luggage people carry is black? Most likely you will have black company-issued luggage as well. In my experience from company to company, all flight attendants carry the same brand of luggage or something very similar. There is nothing to differentiate your bag from the next. Be sure to mark all bags with identification tags however, I find this is not always enough to separate your bag from somebody else's. I have matching teal bows on all three of my bags so they are easily identifiable in the pile of blackness when we get to the hotel or to the airport in the morning. If bows aren't your thing, find a way to mark all of your bags in a similar manner. I took labeling my bag one step further.

Here's a little story.... At the end of the flight one night I was helping the very last passenger out of the back of the plane. After assisting the passenger I went back to get my luggage off the plane. My large roller bag was nowhere to be found. I couldn't believe it. The top of my bag had a giant pink flower and a lime green tag that said crew on it and the passenger still walked away with it. Passengers will see a black bag in their area and automatically assume it's theirs without thoroughly checking the bag. I have seen bags get confused frequently. Fortunately by the time the passenger got halfway down the terminal they realized that my bag was indeed not theirs and they returned it to the gate. I would've been in a world of hurt if I didn't get that bag back. It had my entire universe inside.

LABEL EVERYTHING!

As soon as I got home from that trip I decided to mark my bag in a way that no one would **ever** be able to confuse it with theirs. I went and bought neon pink paint and painted the words "NOT YOURS" in big bold letters underneath the bag. Why I say underneath the bag is because when I put my bag in the overhead bin I make sure the wheels are facing out. This way when everybody walks by to grab their luggage they can see the big bold letters and know the bag is not theirs.

CREATE A SYSTEM

Do things exactly the same way every single time. Become a creature of habit in this job. Put your bag in the same overhead bin every flight. Put your wallet in the same pocket. When you take your apron off, put it back where it belongs. It'll be that one time you do something differently that you will forget something on the plane or in the hotel.

HAVE TWO OF EVERYTHING

I used to repackage all of my toiletries every time I took a trip, but that quickly got old and I often forgot something. Pack a toiletry bag that never leaves your suitcase. Just switch out items when you are in need. Phone chargers are another thing you **must** keep two of. Keep one at home and one in your bag at all times. You don't want to get stuck out on a trip without a phone charger and a dead phone. However, you can find inexpensive chargers almost anywhere. At this point I keep one at home, one in my car, and at least one in my flight attendant bag. Just in case you are in a situation where you cannot plug in your electronic devices, I would suggest carrying an external battery charger. I found one online that charges my phone up to three times on one charge.

STAY SAFE. PROTECT YOURSELF.

TSA OFFERS SELF-DEFENSE CLASSES

You don't need to go get a black belt in karate, but no matter your age, your size, or whether you're male or female, it is a good idea to learn to protect yourself. You will be traveling to new and unknown places and will often be out on the layover by yourself. When you are away from the hotel keep a constant eye on your surroundings. Keep your head on a swivel and be aware of other people around you.

BE AWARE OF PICKPOCKETS

When traveling in foreign places, especially Europe, violence isn't prominent but the most common thing is pickpocketing. No one wants to spend their layover or vacation trying to cancel credit cards and get new IDs. Most pickpockets are not always big scary men, but can be women and even children as well. Most people don't think of children as dangerous, but don't let your guard down, no matter how young and innocent someone may seem. Most will work in pairs or groups, one to distract you and another to pick your pockets. They are often well dressed and you'd never expect them to be thieves. Beware of people on the streets trying to get you to sign petitions for the homeless or the needy or of any kind. One person distracts you to sign a petition while their partner swings around your side or your back and pulls items from your pockets or purse.

IT HAPPENED TO ME . . .

My cousin and I had taken a trip to Paris. A lady and a man were trying to get us to sign their petition. We refused and kept walking. The lady reached around my side trying to stop or slow me down. My cousin walked a few steps ahead of me ignoring the man. We refused and kept walking. The lady then reached around my side trying to stop or slow me down. As soon as she was a few steps ahead of him the man reached into her pocket and pulled out her cell phone without her even knowing. Because I was a few steps behind I was able to see it happen. I could tell the lady was trying to fish for my purse but it was a small bag underneath my coat and she couldn't find it. I pushed the lady off of me and started yelling at the man, "You took her phone! You took her phone!" The man had taken my cousin's phone and placed it on his clipboard and then placed another piece of paper on top of it so no one could see. I ripped the paper off his clipboard and took the phone back and ran up to my cousin. All along she had no idea what had just happened.

Men, keep your wallets in your front pocket. It's harder to pick from the front pocket than a back pocket. Avoid carrying backpacks on your back. It is easy for a thief to open a back zipper without you even knowing. Ladies, if you carry a purse, carry a small handbag with the strap across the body. If it is cold out I would suggest putting your purse across your body first and then put your coat over it so it is not visible to the public. There are various undergarment wallets or money holders out there. Find one that will work and be comfortable for you.

The new thing in theft is to scan your credit or debit cards without even taking them out of your pockets. Thieves have come up with scanning devices to pull your information off your cards just by walking by. There are credit card covers or even little devices to put in your wallet that will protect your cards from getting scanned.

INTERNATIONAL TRIPS

If you are lucky enough to get an international trip as a new hire or even within your first few years of flying, don't let those "senior mammas" push you around. Many will ask "How did you get this trip?" Answer back, "Same way as you, from scheduling." International trips go very senior. Many people who have been working 30-40 years are the ones who have first pick at international trips. If your base has many international flights a day it is more likely you will be able to get one or pick one up. If your base only has a couple international flights a day, you might go an eternity before seeing one.

Once in a while you will get a senior mamma or papa who will try to push you around or bully you. International trips are a lot of work and there is constant hustle and bustle. Once you find out what position you are working on the airplane, consult your flight attendant manual and familiarize yourself with the duties related to that position. Each one is a little different. Don't be afraid to ask for help. Often times you will find that the other flight attendants are very helpful and kind, especially once they find out you are new or newer to international flying.

LET'S $ GET PAID!

Flight attendants are only paid when the airplane door closes until the time the doors open again. Flight attendants are <u>not</u> paid when they check in an hour prior to their flight and they are not paid during the boarding process.

For the first time in the last decade, airlines are finally turning a profit, however, it isn't always reflected in employee pay. Due to rising industry standards, many airlines are raising wages for their flight attendants. Now is the best time ever to become a flight attendant. The first four years working as a flight attendant can seem a little tight as far as pay goes. While the starting pay has risen in recent years, it's still not fantastic money.

Once you hit your fifth year of work, there will most likely be a large jump in pay. If you get discouraged with your paycheck, hang in there. There's a jump in site. In that fifth year, the income becomes more sustainable. The airline should offer a way to keep track of the flights you've worked. Use this to verify that the company has properly added up your hours worked. I have found discrepancies in the past that would have shorted me hundreds of dollars on a paycheck. Every dollar counts! It's your responsibility to ensure the airline is doing things correctly. Believe me, they aren't going to correct anything that you don't catch!

<u>1st Year</u>
$21 to $24 per hour
$18,900 to $21,600 per year

<u>5th Year</u>
$30 to $32 per hour
$27,000 to $28,000 per year

-Based on 75 hours of flying per month as a national average. May not be exact for your airline.

-This does not include additional pay such as lead pay, per diem, or other miscellaneous items you may get paid for.

LEAD PAY

If you work as the lead flight attendant on your trip, you could be paid an additional amount of money per hour. This also involves more responsibilities on each flight.

PER DIEM

Per Diem is a daily or hourly allowance for expenses and items such as food. Airlines will pay you a small hourly rate for each hour you are on your layover. It may not sound like much, but it's an average of $2 an hour you are away from the airplane, which will help offset the cost of any food you buy during your trip.

LOOKING FOR WAYS TO EARN EXTRA INCOME?

WORK ON DAYS OFF

Unless you are able to work out a special or flexible deal, finding a second job and form of income can be very difficult as a flight attendant. Most employers will want you to commit to a schedule. You can work on your days off, but that may not give you much time for other things. The best suggestion I can give is to pick up extra trips on your days off. This will pay you above and beyond your guaranteed hours if you are on reserve. If you are a block holder, you will almost always be able to control how much or how little you work, thus controlling your income.

CREDIT CARD APPLICATIONS

Many airlines offer an air miles credit card program for their passengers. The programs are offered and distributed by flight attendants during the flight. During the flight, you'll make an announcement about the credit benefits, walk through the cabin handing out applications, collect the applications at the end of the flight and turn them in for processing. If the applications get approved, you will receive $25-$50. Be sure to take advantage of these programs. This could really help your paycheck.

YOU'RE ABOUT TO GET TO KNOW YOUR COWORKERS <u>REALLY</u> WELL!!

It's amazing how much you can learn about people in 1 to 4 days. You are working in a giant metal tube with nowhere to go and sit alone. Therefore, you will get to know your crew members very well by the end of your trip. Guaranteed you will know the following about each of your fellow crew members:

- How long they have been working for the airline
- If they worked for another airline beforehand
- If they were ever laid off from their airline in the past
- How long they served on reserve
- How long they have been married or in a relationship
- How many children and grandchildren they have and where they live
- What kind of trips they like to work and dislike
- Their pet peeves about passengers and flying
- What education they had and where they went to college

FLIGHT BENEFITS

MARRY ME, FLY FOR FREE!

Most likely, your airline will provide free flight benefits to you. This will allow you to commute to and from work or roam the country or even the world as you please. When you travel out of the country, be prepared to pay the taxes to get into that country. For example, it cost me roughly $50 to get into Italy and nearly $200 to get into England. We have this little saying in the airlines about marrying me so you can fly for free! Well, it *should* read, "Marry me and fly standby!" Well, what if you're not married? Don't worry, most likely your airline will have an option for those awesomely single people out there we call a "registered guest." This person can be a spouse, a boyfriend, a girlfriend, or even a friend. Each airline does it a little differently, but registered guests pay only a small fee or tax per flight. These taxes or fees may come directly out of your own paycheck. It's a good idea to keep track of how much that person is flying so you know how much will be coming out of your paycheck each time. It's generally minimal enough with each flight that it shouldn't make too big of a difference in your paycheck, but it can add up.

If you need to take this person off of your benefits, inform your company right away and change the passwords to your flight account if possible.

BUDDY PASSES

Once people find out you are a flight attendant, one of the first questions they will ask you is "Do you have buddy passes?" When the economy took a turn for the worse, a few companies did away with their buddy pass program. Check with your airline.

For those who still have buddy passes, it can be a difficult process. Years ago, flying standby was a breeze and there were almost always seats open for non-revenue passengers. Nowadays, flights are more frequently completely booked. However there's always a chance that a connecting flight will get delayed and passengers won't make their next flight, leaving seats open for non-revs.

These are not free tickets, but stand-by tickets at a fraction of the cost of full-priced tickets. Warn your friends and family ahead of time that this is a "STANDY-BY" ticket and there aren't any guarantees that they will make the flight. Cross your fingers and hope everyone makes it on without a hitch.

Anyone who flies on your flight benefits is a direct representation of YOU. If a person traveling on your benefits misbehaves or gets themselves into trouble, you will be held directly responsible and could lose your flight benefits entirely, even if you aren't traveling with that person. Warn them to be on their best behavior and to dress appropriately.

If your guest does not make their original flight, encourage them to be patient and to talk to the gate agent. There may be very little that you can do to assist them at that point. Have them prepare to spend the day, if not the night, in the airport in the unfortunate case that they cannot make it onto a flight right away.

CHILDREN

Depending on the airline, your children will be able to fly up until the age of 24 or so. Again, you will pay taxes on their flights. Children under the age of two do not need their own seat, therefore you won't be charged anything for them.

PARENTS

Parents are often in a category of their own. Parents will generally be charged a small amount per mile they fly or one standard fee per one way they fly. Double check with your airline what these charges may be.

DO YOU TRUST THIS PERSON TO BE ON THEIR BEST BEHAVIOR?

IF A BUDDY PASS RIDER GETS IN TROUBLE, YOU COULD LOSE ALL FLYING PRIVILEGES

DON'T EVER SELL YOUR BUDDY PASSES FOR A PROFIT

ELIGIBLE AGE FOR CHILDREN OR DEPENDENTS IS 2-24

TRACK YOUR FLYING!

Start a spreadsheet of all the flights you take as a passenger and keep a running tally of how much money you would have spent if you had to pay for all those flights. Within my first year and a half of flying I used over $30,000 of flight benefits for FREE!!! Holy Moly! Who spends 30K in flights a year? Not me!

Another great thing I found is a website called www.FlightDiary.net where you can go and enter all your flying, both personal and professional, and it will add up all your miles, keep track of where you've been and which routes you have taken.

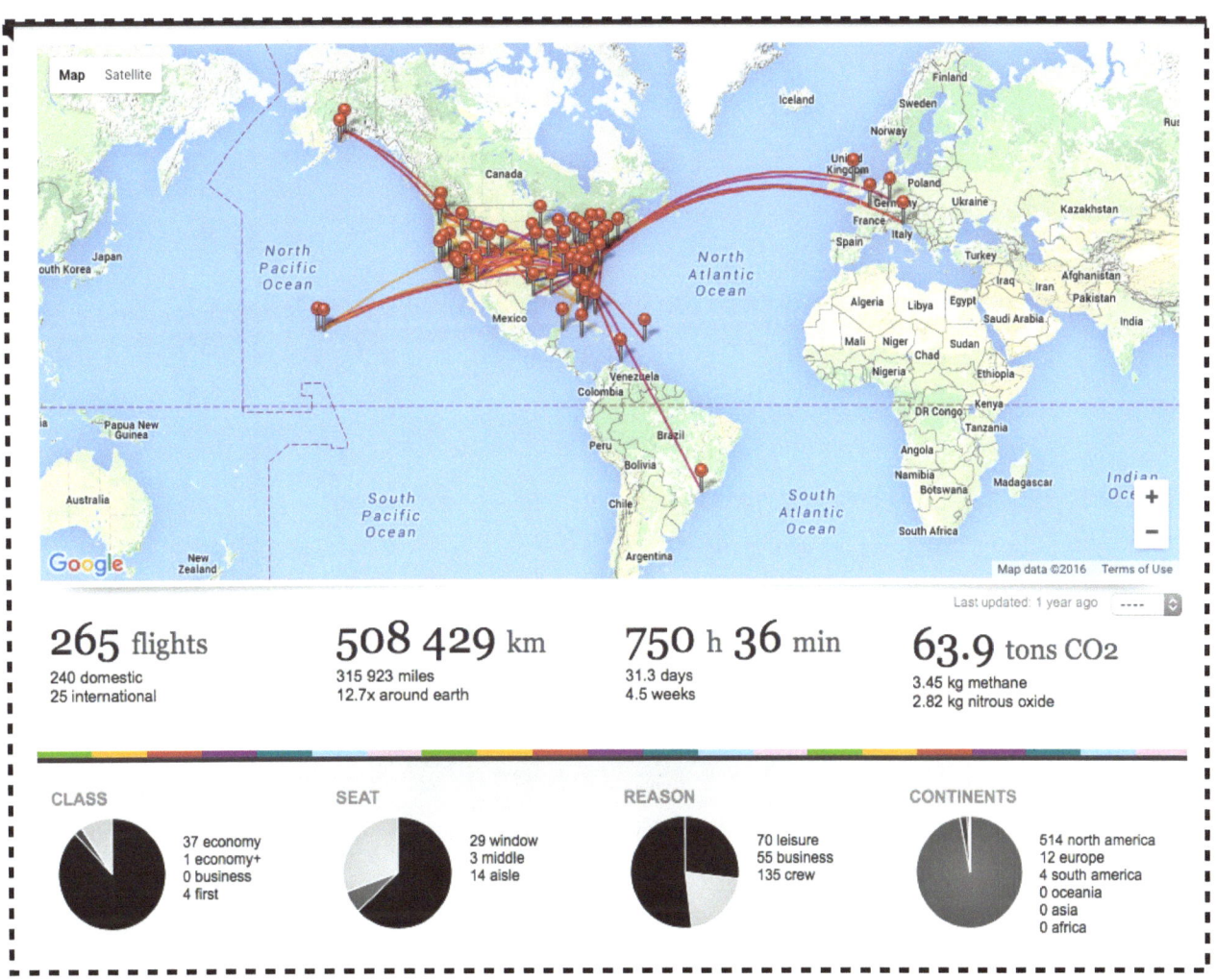

THE RESERVE FLIGHT ATTENDANT

WELCOME TO THE LIFE OF BEING ON "RESERVE"

As a reserve flight attendant, you are on call for several days in a row and hang out in your base city until scheduling calls you with a trip. Airlines will keep a percentage of their flight attendants on call each day to fill in for other flight attendants when they call in sick, get stuck somewhere, or if a previous flight cancels and they need a new crew to work the next flight out. You never know where you'll end up that day!

HOW LONG WILL I BE ON RESERVE?

You're starting the job at the most perfect time! After 9/11, airlines didn't hire for nearly 10 years. This meant that the flight attendants that were at the bottom of the seniority list had to stay at the bottom because there weren't any new people coming in behind them. These flight attendants who were on reserve had to stay on reserve for upwards of 15-18 years. I don't know how those people did it. Being on reserve is interesting enough, but having to stay on reserve for nearly two decades would not be my idea of fun. Now that airlines across the United States are hiring like crazy, it's possible that you will be on reserve for 6 months to 3 years.

FLY BY THE SEAT OF YOUR PANTS

Each airline does things a little differently. Some airlines offer a revolving reserve program, meaning that you will serve a month on reserve and the next month as a block holder (meaning you have a set schedule each month) and it will alternate. Some will vary on how many months of each you will serve before alternating. *Example:* One month on reserve and three months as a block holder.

Being on reserve means that you will be literally flying through life by the seat of your pants. You never know when you're going to get called out. Okay, that may not be entirely true. Scheduling will post online what number you are to be called out, but when they do call you need to be ready to drop everything and get to the airport by check-in time. Scheduling can give you a minimum of two hours to make it to the gate from the time they call.

"What number am I?" The number one thing on your mind when you wake up each morning will be, "What number am I to be called out?" It'll get to the point where your friends and family will know to ask you that question each time they talk to you, hang out with you or make plans with you. You'll find yourself checking your schedule multiple times a day. Somedays you can be number 2 all day and never get called out or you could be number 30 and the company will have a crazy day and they will go through reserve flight attendants left and right and you'll eventually get called out. Each day is unpredictable. If there is severe weather, you can almost plan on having to take a trip that day or the next.

There is nothing predictable about being on reserve. As soon as you think you have everything in the system figured out, something will catch you off guard.

How do I check my number? Many airlines have a computer system or even a phone app where you can find and track what number you are to be called out and what trips are available.

SCHEDULING

DEALING WITH SCHEDULING

During flight attendant training, I was basically taught to fear scheduling when they called and to never argue with them. Please, please, please learn from me and **never** fear scheduling. If there is something that you feel you are being unfairly assigned, don't hesitate to ask to speak to a supervisor before accepting the trip. If you were wrong in your assumption, then the worst that could happen is that you have to take your trip. If you are right in feeling that things were unfair, a supervisor may correct the mistake. In my experience, the supervisors are far friendlier than the schedulers themselves. Be calm and be kind when asking for a supervisor.

One time I was assigned a trip that I thought I was not eligible for. I kindly asked for a supervisor. He explained that the details of my flight attendant contract said that they could indeed assign me the trip and what the reasons were. Two days later I was contacted by scheduling for a similar kind of trip, but because I knew the details of my contract, I was able to instruct scheduling that the particular trip they were trying to assign me did not fit within those parameters. The scheduler put me on hold for a moment and when she returned, she told me that I was correct and that I didn't have to take that trip.

It was a really good thing I knew the details of what they could and couldn't do. I immediately sent out a mass text to the flight attendants next on the list to let them know what scheduling was trying to pull. My text ended up saving other flight attendants who did not know that particular detail.

DAILY SCHEDULING

Your airline will have a department called "Daily Scheduling" that manages all the flights going out and the flight attendants that need to cover open trips.

FUTURE SCHEDULING

Future Scheduling is the department at your airline that manages and fills all the trips that open up for the next day. Airlines don't like delays or cancellations so they will be sure to fill positions as far ahead of time as possible.

If they get to you, scheduling might either call you and ask you what trip you want for the following day or assign you what trip is left. Some companies will allow you to bid online the day before for what you want to do the next day. Options may include taking a trip or remaining on call for the next day. One benefit to being assigned a trip the day before is that you will have sufficient time to plan, pack, and make food enough for the duration of your trip. If you don't like being blasted out of bed at 5:00am by a scheduling call each day, I would suggest taking a trip from future scheduling. If there isn't a trip that you want, then take your chances and see what kind of trip you get the next day, if any, or leave a list of the kinds of trips you would like them to call you back with should more trips open up.

LEAVE A LIST OF TRIPS YOU WANT!

If scheduling calls you and they don't have a trip you are legal for, you may often leave a wish list of the type of trip you would like them to call you back with.

The first time scheduling asked me if I wanted to leave a list, this is how the conversation went:

Scheduler: "What are your parameters?"
Me: "I don't understand, what are you asking me for?"
Scheduler: "What are your parameters for your list?"
Me: "What kinds of things can I ask for?"
Scheduler: "Anything, what are your parameters?"
Me: "Call me back if you have a Denver trip."
Scheduler: "That's not a proper parameter. What else do you want to ask for?"
Me: "I still have no idea what you are looking for me to say, so I'll just leave it to chance."

End of **THAT** conversation.

Get familiar with what they are asking for. You might be able to say:
   "I want any two or three day trip that departs after 1300 tomorrow."
   "I want any one day trip in by 1800 tomorrow."

*See page 87 for more information the 24-hour clock.

By knowing what scheduling is looking for when you leave a list, you can start to slightly control your schedule. There is no guarantee you will get what you asked for, but they will try to fulfill requests to those who have left a list before moving on to those who have not. Whether you are on reserve or a block holder, you can always leave a list.

OPEN TIME

Open time is the list of flights that are currently available and need to be covered. Block holders have first pick from these trips, and what is left is assigned to reserve flight attendants. Some airlines allow you to pick from the list which trip you prefer and other airlines will assign you a trip based on criteria such as how many days you are available or which trip leaves first. Be sure to know your contract if you have one and what kind of rights you have when being assigned or picking a trip. Many flight attendants don't know their contract and scheduling has taken advantage of them and assigned them trips they never should have received.

TRADE BOARD

When you are on reserve, you should be able to pick up extra trips on your days off if you are "legal" to work them. Legal means you are eligible to work the trip based on parameters such as how many days in a row you are allowed to work according to company restrictions. Check with your airline for more details on this. A trade board is usually offered online and shows lists of trips that other flight attendants are trying to get rid of or trade.

ON-PREMISE RESERVE

Most flight attendants that are on call are allowed to continue on with their lives at home in their base city until they are called or needed. On-Premise Reserve is a flight attendant who is assigned to sit at the airport for roughly 3-5 hours in case the airline needs you to be on the airplane within minutes to ensure an on-time departure. If they assign you a trip, you go. If they don't assign you a trip during that time and your time is up, you are free to go home.

Bring something to entertain yourself because on-premise reserve can get very boring. Pack a snack, too. I always bring my headphones and iPad to keep myself busy. My airport has a lounge area in the crew room, and depending on the time of day, I might sleep in the lazy-boy chair until I get a call.

Packing: If you are assigned on-premise reserve, be sure to pack your bags for every type of weather, both cold and hot depending on the time of year. Pack enough clothes for several days because you won't know how many days you will be gone until they assign you a trip. One time in January, I was assigned a trip that had layovers in Miami, Florida and Buffalo, New York. I needed both shorts and a snow parka for that trip.

Food: If you are trying to eat healthy or avoid spending money on dining out, pack enough food for several days. If you don't get a trip, they you can take the food home.

SUMMERS ON RESERVE

I hope you are ready to fly your little wings off! During the summer, if you are on reserve, plan on flying almost every day that you are on call. Most summers that I've been on call, I've flown almost every day from May 15 to August 31. Why do you fly so much in the summer? Kids are off school during the summer and block holders who are parents will tend to call in sick, take personal days, or will have vacation days to be home with their children. Airlines also offer many more flights a day and need more coverage. Because there are more flights during the summer, there is a greater possibility that you might be awarded a set schedule or line for one or more of the summer months. It's never a guarantee though. Paychecks will be larger during the summer due to the additional per diem pay and the extra little things that airlines may pay you for.

WINTERS ON RESERVE

I hope you have a monthly subscription to Netflix or Hulu! Be prepared to sit on your hands most of the winter months. My first winter on reserve I binge watched Netflix for hours a day. The winters after that I rationed my binge watching and made sure to get active and find hobbies. October is a moderate flying month, but November through February you can count on flying maybe two trips a month. If you get bored, you always have the option of calling scheduling and telling them you want to fly. They'll put you on the "quick call" or "aggressive" list and call you when a trip pops up.

BENEFITS OF BEING ON RESERVE

Some people don't mind being on reserve and other's won't like it at all. The time of year can affect that as well. One of the benefits of being on reserve is getting really good trips once in a while that might not have been awarded to you having such junior seniority. International flights are always awarded to line holders who have 35-40 years of seniority. If one of them should call out sick at the very last minute, a reserve will be called out to work the flight. During the summer, it's very common for reserve flight attendants to get international trips.

PAY WHILE ON RESERVE

There will be many months where you will only fly 40 to 50 hours a month. That's not a whole lot and a person can't survive only being paid for that little. While you are on reserve, you will have a guaranteed paycheck of roughly 75 hours a month whether you fly one hour or 75 hours. That number will differ between airlines, but it's an average. The average flight attendant flies 75-105 hours a month when they are line holders. Remember that things such as per diem, lead flight attendant pay, and other things contribute to your paycheck when you fly.

HAVE QUESTIONS?

If at any time you don't understand something about scheduling or how schedules work, one of your best resources is going to be other flight attendants, more particularly ones that are more senior to you and have learned things along the way. Senior Mammas have been doing this a very long time and they have learned a lot of tricks of the trade. You can learn loop holes and secrets from others. Also, join a Facebook page for the flight attendants at your airline. There is a ton of instant help there. Everyone else is in the same boat (or plane per say!). Someone else may post a question that you've never thought to ask. Watch as the replies instantly pour in.

LINE-HOLDER

Becoming a Line Holder is what every flight attendant dreams of.

Seniority is everything in the airlines. It dictates what kind of destinations and schedules you get. We've covered the life of being on reserve, but now let's get to the good stuff.

Having a "line" or becoming a "line holder" changes your entire world. If there are enough trips for the month and you are senior enough you will be awarded a line or a set schedule for the entire month, sometimes two months in advance depending on your scheduling system. Line holders are able to bid for the type of trip, how long they want to be gone, where they want to go, and how many hours they want to work. Those with the most seniority will get top pick and those at the bottom of the food chain will get what's left over. Believe me when I say a "bad" schedule is better than no schedule. Even if you are awarded a schedule that you don't like or there are trips that you are not fond of, it's not the end of the world. There are options for trading, dropping, or swapping your trips.

How long until I can become a line holder and get a schedule?

After September 11, 2011, airlines went on a hiring freeze for nearly a decade. Flight attendants who were hired prior to that went upward of 10-15 years before becoming a line holder. The average time now is 6 months to 3 years to move up to line holder status.

BIDDING FOR TRIPS

A line holder, or a block holder (the term is interchangeable), is a flight attendant who is senior enough to bid for and receive a set schedule each month. Line holders bid for specific kinds of trips they want and on what days. The schedule you receive for that month is called your "line". You may not always get the exact trips you want, but you will know a month in advance what your schedule will be. You'll know what day the trip leaves, what day it comes back, where you'll be staying, and for how long.

TRADING TRIPS

Line holders may trade their trips with other line holders. Some airlines offer you the choice to change your trip out for another trip that is open on the daily schedule.

CALLING IN SICK

When a line holder calls in sick, another line holder may pick-up that trip off the daily schedule or a reserve flight attendant will be called out to cover the trip.

DEALING WITH SCHEDULING

In my experience as a line holder, schedulers are much nicer to me when I call than when I was on reserve. You might be able to call scheduling and leave a list of the trips you want if you are trying to swap out for something you already have.

LEARN TIPS AND TRICKS

Every scheduling system has its loop holes, and there are ways to manipulate things in order to make your schedule work best for you. Each person has their own needs and preferences and you will find what works for you. There is no handbook when you go from a reserve flight attendant to a line holder. The best bet is to ask fellow flight attendants, especially those more senior to you, how they bid or work their schedule in their best interest.

YOUR PERSONAL LIFE

FAMILY LIFE & SUPPORT

Before you dive into the lengthy process of becoming a flight attendant, let's get personal. Being a flight attendant is not just a job, but a lifestyle. Take time to think about your personal life and your work-life balance. It's incredibly important that you have family or a support system who will back you up in the flight attendant lifestyle. It's a different kind of life for sure, but the benefits can be wonderful. Here are some things to consider…

- Are you married?

- Will your spouse support your traveling work lifestyle?

- Are you in a relationship?

- How will traveling affect your dating/married life?

- Will your family understand if you have to miss a birthday party or special event due to having to work?

- Do you have children?

- Are you willing to leave your children for 1-4 days at a time?

- Do you have support in raising them, getting them to school, getting them tucked into bed, etc.?

- Training will be several weeks long. Can your family manage for that length of time without you there?

- Are you willing or able to drop everything and go if scheduling calls you? (While on reserve)

WEEKENDS

Most likely you will start your flight attendant career by being on reserve the first few months or possibly even the first few years. As a reserve flight attendant you will be at the bottom of the totem pole and you will be awarded your pick of monthly schedules last (and you'll receive what's left over). Improving your seniority depends on how many people the airline hires after you. This means you will most likely be working a lot of weekends. However, some people are able to hold weekends off after 8 or 9 months of hire.

HOLIDAYS

When you first start, expect to work most holidays, especially Thanksgiving, Christmas, and New Year's. Oddly enough, Halloween is one of the biggest days for block holders to call in sick therefore, reserve flight attendants end up being called out to fill those positions. The upside of having to work holidays that you have four or more other crew members including pilots in the same boat as you. They will most likely want to go out as a group and celebrate together. However, there *will* be a ton of trip options to choose from. I once got a trip that took me back to my home town for Christmas Eve. I got paid to go home for the holiday!

SPECIAL EVENTS

There will be times when you plan to make it to a birthday party or event and then get called out at the last minute or can't get someone to cover your trip. Bummer, right? But on the upside, since you fly for free or next to it, you will also have the chance to fly around the country and make it to events that you wouldn't be able to if you had a "normal" job. For goodness sakes, who gets to fly across the country to make it to a friend's baby shower of all things? Pretty cool right? Where else do you get to have that kind of option (FOR FREE)?

When you are grumpy and super disappointed that you have to be driving to the airport right now and you're missing that super cool event, remember that you have a pretty sweet job, an awesome life, and you've been able to make it to things that most people wouldn't be able to.

-LIFE BALANCE-

Make a List of Your Own Pros & Cons

Every person has different needs in their lives.
Make a list of the pros and cons about becoming a flight attendant.

PROS	CONS

DO YOU HAVE WHAT IT TAKES?

- Do you love working with people?
- Do you have interest in aviation?
- Can you be polite even in frustrating situations?
- Do you enjoy having every day being different?
- Can you handle unpredictable days?
- Do you handle exploring alone while on trips?
- Do you make new friends easily?
- Can you work with new people every trip?
- Can you smile even when you don't feel like it?
- Can you improvise?

What kinds of characteristics do YOU think it takes to be a good flight attendant?
(Hint - this could be a question asked at your interview)

*Use adjectives and full sentences!

- _____
- _____
- _____

YOUR TICKET TO THE INTERVIEW!

LET'S SET UP YOUR RESUME

Your resume is your ticket to getting an interview. You could be the most qualified person in the world for the job, but if your resume is lacking, you could miss out on your chance for the job that is right for you!

One of the hardest things to do is to get the ball rolling and to start your resume. What if you've never been a flight attendant before or have never worked in a customer service industry? Don't sweat, there are ways to write your resume to cater to the flight attendant application.

PREVIOUS EXPERIENCE

You don't have to have any previous experience as a flight attendant to get hired with the airlines. Many airlines will hire straight out of college as well. If you do have previous experience working as a flight attendant, do NOT mention that to other people interviewing along with you. They will latch on to you and ask you *all day* about what it's like to work as a flight attendant and it will take away from your ability to shine in the interview with that company. I've seen it happen before. You may miss out on a new opportunity with a new airline.

As a flight attendant you will be the face of the airline and your job will be all about customer service. Do you have any customer service experience? Even if you don't have any customer service experience, there are ways to highlight key things about your past work experience that will show you are qualified for the job.

LET'S HIGHLIGHT THINGS ABOUT YOU OTHER THAN YOUR WORK EXPERIENCE!

Personality Traits:

_____   _____

_____   _____

Leadership Skills:

_____   _____

_____   _____

Safety/Precaution Training:

_____   _____

_____   _____

Service Skills:

_____   _____

_____   _____

Related Course Work:
(Any courses that provided you with skills which will be beneficial to being a flight attendant.)

_____   _____

_____   _____

Highlighting your skills before stating your work history may seem a little untraditional, but employers are looking for key things that make you stand out. If your work history is not the item that stands out the most, highlight your skills. Don't be shy! *Now is the time to brag about yourself.* Have someone else glance over your resume to ensure that it all makes sense and is an easy read. Here is a small example of how you can set up your resume. Be sure to go far more in depth than this one. Don't just copy and paste what the employer is looking for.

Emery Britain
123 Main Street
Anywhere, USA 12345
(303) 555-5555   emery.britain@email.com

Personality — Cheerful person who loves to work with customers and making them feel comfortable in their environment. Likes to build relationships with those around. Very organized and able to multi-task.

Leadership — Confident in communicating with customers and coworkers. Takes initiative to solve problems and troubleshoot.

Safety — CPR & First Aid certified

Service — Always on time to work. Delivers excellent customer service. Works well as a team with others and can complete individual tasks in a timely manner. Listens to others' needs and strives to meet those needs to the best of ability.

Work Experience

Hobby Ville – *Cashier*
2015 - Present
Provided excellent customer service at the cashier counter. Answered all customer questions with a smile. Helped customers identify the right product for their needs.

Collegiate Event Planner – *Catering Intern*
2010 - 2014
Set up and tear down for University events. Responsible for on-time delivery of event equipment.

Education — University of Somewhere - B.A in Underwater Basket Weaving
2010-2014

Awards — 2016 Colorado Figure Skating Club- Ice skater of the year award

WHICH AIRLINE DO YOU WANT TO APPLY FOR?

DON'T PICK JUST ONE!

GIVE YOURSELF OPTIONS!

AIRLINE NAME	ARE THEY MAINLINE OR REGIONAL?
_____ →	_____
_____ →	_____
_____ →	_____
_____ →	_____
_____ →	_____
_____ →	_____

GET TO KNOW YOUR AIRLINE

DO YOUR RESEARCH!

Your interviewer(s) will expect you to know quite a bit about their company. Find out as many key or interesting details as you can about the airline you are looking to get hired by.

Name of airline: _____

Is this a "Mainline" or "Regional" airline? _____

How long has the airline been in business? _____

How did this airline start? _____

What airlines have they merged with in the past? _____

Do they have international flights? _____

Where are their bases? _____

Are they part of a travel alliance? _____

Other Information: _____

_____

GET TO KNOW YOUR AIRLINE

DO YOUR RESEARCH!

Name of airline: _____

Is this a "Mainline" or "Regional" airline? _____

How long has the airline been in business? _____

How did this airline start? _____

What airlines have they merged with in the past? _____

Do they have international flights? _____

Where are their bases? _____

Are they part of a travel alliance? _____

Other Information: _____

_____

_____

GET TO KNOW YOUR AIRLINE

DO YOUR RESEARCH!

Name of airline: _____

Is this a "Mainline" or "Regional" airline? _____

How long has the airline been in business? _____

How did this airline start? _____

What airlines have they merged with in the past? _____

Do they have international flights? _____

Where are their bases? _____

Are they part of a travel alliance? _____

Other Information: _____

_____

_____

PUT YOUR BEST FOOT FORWARD

HOW TO DRESS FOR THE INTERVIEW

Admit it, when you are wearing a sassy outfit, you feel as if you could conquer the world and nothing is going to stand in your way. You carry yourself just a little taller when you know you look good. How you are dressed also says a lot about you. In fact it's the first impression you give to other people. When you are getting ready for your interview, think about the last time you saw a group of flight attendants walking down the terminal at the airport. I bet you didn't take your eyes off of them for even a second. They all looked so put together and you wished in that moment that you could have their lives jetting all over the world and getting paid for it too. Those flight attendants were probably the most glamorous working people you've ever laid eyes on. Now it's your turn to be as pressed and dressed as those flight attendants. Airlines are looking for people who know how to dress and take care of themselves. Flight attendants come in all shapes, sizes and colors. No matter what your physical attributes are, it's time to dress like you own the skies! Let's plan out your outfit for the interview and rock what your mamma gave ya! It's possible to be stunning while staying professional. Professional business attire is a must! You are going to a flight attendant interview, so it's time to dress like one!

YOU NEVER GET A SECOND CHANCE TO MAKE A FIRST IMPRESSION!

HAIR STYLE

For Guys: No long hair will be allowed. As a general rule of thumb, make sure your hair is cut short enough so that it's not touching your shirt collar.

For Gals: Hairstyles should be kept professional. No exotic or edgy hairstyles should be worn to the interview or to work. Bangs or fringe should be short enough so that it doesn't fall into your eyes or go lower than your eyebrows. Make sure your hairstyle won't cause you to constantly be brushing hair away from your face or your eyes. The interviewers will be looking at that. If your hair is pulled back, use hair spray to get rid of any "whispies". During training, some airlines are known to ding you for having "whispies" and you will be told to go take care of them immediately. Bobby pins will also become your new best friend. One test to make sure your hairstyle is good to go: bow your head down, if the hair stays off your face, then you should be okay. You may have to bend down to pick something up out of your cart or off a passenger's tray table. You don't want to be dealing with hair in your face when you are serving food, ever.

HAIR COLOR

Natural looking hair colors are a must. If you have extreme colors in your hair, I would suggest changing it before the interview. It won't be allowed on the job.

FACIAL HAIR

It's okay for guys to have facial hair such as beards, goatees, and mustaches - just be sure they are trimmed short and clean. No long beards like "father time". You'll want to be trimmed and professional. Double check with your airline on their facial hair policy.

PIERCINGS

For Guys: I would strongly recommend removing ALL earrings for this interview. Most likely you won't be able to wear them on the job.

For Gals: As a rule of thumb, keep your earrings to the size of a quarter or smaller. If you have multiple piercings, keep it to one earring in each ear. If you have piercings anywhere on your ear other than on the lobe, take it out.

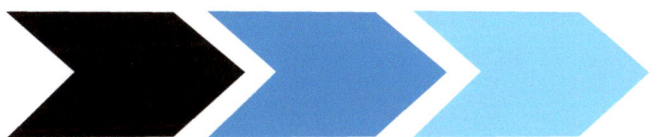

JEWELRY

Wearing jewelry is okay, but be sure you're not wearing anything too big, too much or something that is over the top.

Rings: No more than 2 rings per hand. Too many rings and your hands attract too much awkward attention.

Necklaces: Keep it simple. Wear one necklace and not too long.

Bracelets: Wear one bracelet. Make sure it doesn't make too much noise when you move your hands around.

MAKEUP

For Gals: Makeup will be a requirement for working on an airplane. Depending on the airline, it generally consists of mascara, lipstick and blush. When you are getting ready for the interview, I would wear at least those three things. Don't go overboard though. Make sure the makeup you wear is tasteful.

Lipstick: Shades should be kept in pinks, reds, and neutrals. During training, be sure your lipstick or gloss is always fresh. They will be keeping an eye on your personal appearance the whole time. Some airlines are known to tell you to fix your lips if the color has worn off.

For Guys: Makeup of any kind should not be worn.

PERFUME OR COLOGNE

GO EASY ON THE STUFF!!!! One shot of perfume is enough. You want to smell nice, but you don't want to be the person who walks in the room and leaves a trail of scent behind you. Remember, just because you like your perfume, does not mean that everyone will be a fan of it as well. Often time people will have allergic reactions to strong scents so please go easy on the perfume and cologne. You wouldn't want to be stuck in cramped quarters on the airplane next to someone who has a really strong scent on. Keep that in mind when getting ready for your interview.

WRIST WATCH

You'll be required to wear a working wrist watch everyday on the job. I can't tell you how many times a day you'll be asked on the airplane, "What time is it?" or "How much longer do we have until we land?" You'll need a watch to be able to answer this. Wear one to your interview.

FINGERNAILS

For Guys: Should be kept trimmed and clean.

For Gals: Whether your nails are real or fake, they should be kept all the same length, but not too long. Colors should be kept in pinks, reds, and neutrals. No extreme colors or designs.

TATTOOS

Visible tattoos are not going to fly well with most airlines. If you have tattoos on your arms, be sure to wear long sleeves to the interview. It could be 110 degrees in Phoenix but I guarantee you the people conducting the interview will not want to see tattoos on your arms. Cover up. When you are working on the airplane you will be required to wear uniforms that cover visible tattoos as well. If you have one around your wrist that you are afraid will show, I would suggest getting something flesh colored to cover it such as a moleskin or a Band-Aid. Wearing a watch or a bracelet wouldn't hurt either, just make sure it's not too flashy.

SHOES

For Guys: Dress shoes in black, brown, or navy are appropriate for the interview. No tennis shoes or sandals.

For Gals: Whether you plan to wear dress slacks or a skirt, I would highly recommend wearing closed toe heels. Heel height should be from 1" to 3". Do not wear heels higher than 3". Believe me, you wouldn't want to wear super high heels on the airplane, especially when your balance can easily be swayed on the airplane due to any slight turbulence. Leave the clubbing shoes at home. No tennis shoes, sandals or open-toed shoes.

The airlines can be are very particular about the shoes you wear and the appropriate shoes for each type of uniform outfit. You won't be allowed to wear any shoes with straps, bows, or extra embellishments.

SOCKS & STOCKINGS

For Guys: Socks that match or compliment your shoes and pants.

For Gals: Socks that match your shoes or pants. If you are wearing a skirt, stockings or pantyhose are an absolute must. Avoid any pantyhose that have patterns.

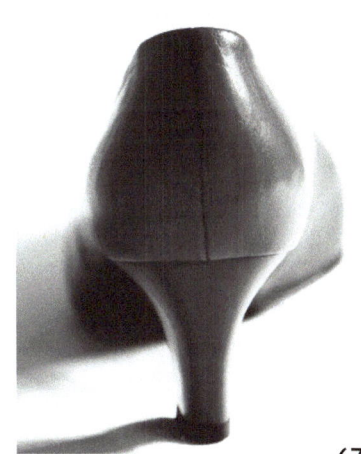

LET'S GET DRESSED!

GUYS
- Button-up Collared Shirt
- Suit Jacket
- Tie
- Clean Shaven or Trimmed Up
- Dress Shoes
- Briefcase or Portfolio
- No Facial Piercings
- Single Earrings in Each Ear
- No Visible Tattoos

GALS
- Dress Blouse
- Dress or Skirt
- Dress Pants
- Pantyhose
- Dress Shoes
- Hair Pulled Back From Face
- No Facial Piercings
- Single Earrings in Each Ear
- No Visible Tattoos

-WHAT TO BRING TO THE INTERVIEW-

- [ ] Chapstick
- [ ] Bottle of Water - Stay Hydrated
- [ ] Note Pad
- [ ] Pen
- [ ] Driver's License
- [ ] Passport
- [ ] Blank Check

BODY LANGUAGE
SPEAKS LOUDER THAN WORDS

WHAT DOES YOUR BODY LANGUAGE SAY ABOUT YOU?

Did you know that how you stand or where you place your arms speaks more about you than the words you say out loud?

NERVOUS BODY LANGUAGE
- Arms crossed
- Eyes down, appearing unsure
- Won't hold eye contact
- Ending sentences with an upward inflection
- Hair twirling
- Constant smiling without break, looking nervous
- Shoulders rolled forward and body slumped
- Weak, limp handshake

CONFIDENT BODY LANGUAGE
- Eyes looking up, around, and aware
- Smile when appropriate
- Make direct-eye contact with people
- Move with fluid motion
- Shoulders rolled back
- Arms are open, wide, and expressive
- Firm handshake

Employers are more likely to hire people who look confident over people who look intimidated even if both candidates had the exact same thing to say.

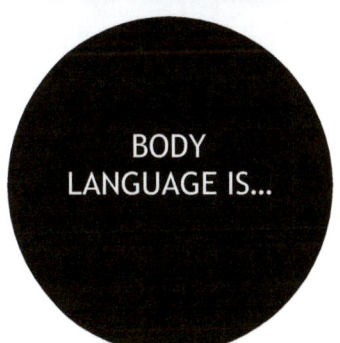

BODY LANGUAGE IS...

7% OF WHAT YOU ACTUALLY SAY

93% OF WHAT YOUR BODY LANGUAGE SAYS

WHAT KIND OF PRESENCE DO YOU HAVE WHEN YOU WALK INTO A ROOM?

Each person who walks into the room has a different kind of presence. In an interview, you want to walk in with a strong and confident presence. Keep in mind all of these factors that go into having a strong presence. Practice sitting, walking, talking, and carrying yourself with all of characteristics above.

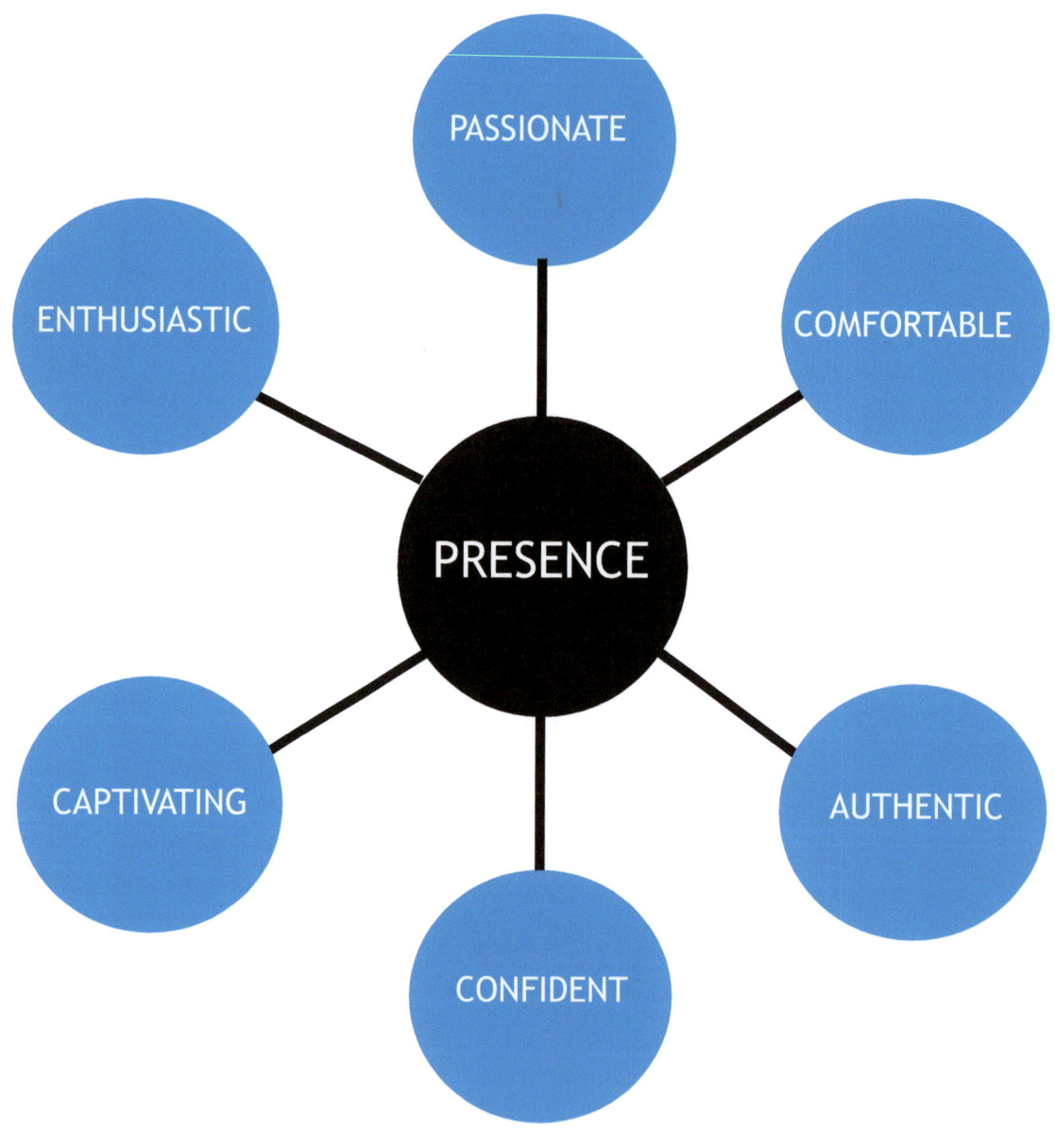

YOU'RE READY FOR THE INTERVIEW!

PHONE INTERVIEW

A representative from the airline (or a third party representing the airline) may call you for a phone interview. They will have many customer service related questions. Treat this just like a normal interview and answer to the best of your ability. Still smile even though the interviewer can't see you. They can still hear the smile in your voice. Be chipper, cheerful, and upbeat.

VIDEO OR SKYPE CHAT

Skype interviews will be one-on-one with an airline representative. Be sure to dress professionally and do your hair. They want to see what you look like as much as they want to know your answers.

RECORDED VIDEO SUBMISSIONS

Video interviews are not always with a person. You will have the opportunity to answer questions while being recorded. You can go back and review your answers before you submit your videos. You may have the chance to re-record your entire video.

TYPES OF INTERVIEWS

PHONE - VIDEO OR SKYPE CHAT - RECORDED VIDEO SUBMISSION
ONE-ON-ONE IN-PERSON - GROUP-FORMAT IN-PERSON

IN-PERSON INTERVIEW

You will go to the airline headquarters or one of the bases and interview in person. There may be both individual and group interviews. Research your airline of choice to see what other people have experienced in previous interviews for that company. From the very first moment you walk in the door and with the very first "Hello", your interview has begun. Every employee in the building might be evaluating you and giving input to the final results.

ONE-ON-ONE INTERVIEW

Here are some of the possibilities for the one-on-one interview:
- Have one interview one-on-one
- Have multiple one-on-one interviews in one day with multiple interviewers
- Interview with a single person
- Interview with a panel of interviewers

GROUP INTERVIEW

There may be several different kinds of group activities throughout the day. Interviewers will be looking at your interactions with other people. If there is a group activity, be fully engaged and participate as much as possible. Be sure to include everyone in the activity. Show leadership, but don't drown out or exclude others. Ask other participants for their input and their opinions. Don't be bossy, but don't be shy.

You will be working in a group atmosphere every single day on that airplane and most likely without a supervisor present. Interviewers use group activities to evaluate your ability to do so.

GOING TO THE INTERVIEW

There's a really good chance that you do not live in the city in which the interview is taking place. If you do, awesome. If you don't, most likely the airline will pay for you to fly out for the in-person interview. Be prepared to wake up incredibly early, fly out on the first flight out, go to the interview, and fly home that evening.

The airline will send you instructions on what to do, where to go, and what to bring.

READ AN ANNOUNCEMENT OUT LOUD

If they give you an announcement card to read out loud, take a moment to read it and familiarize yourself with it. Don't just read the card - PERFORM!

HINT

Think of the last announcement you've heard on an airplane. Use inflection in your voice and sound like you are happy while reading it. Smile, too. People can hear the smile in your voice.

Here is an example:

"Hello! Good morning and welcome! My name is Erika and I'm from Denver, Colorado. I think being a great flight attendant goes beyond serving a soda and pretzels to 175 passengers three times a day. It's about being a good listener, whether that is listening to a distressed passenger or listening to your fellow flight attendant. Maybe that passenger is having a bad day and you might just be the very first delightful smile they've see all day. Be there to calm them and reassure them."

-ALERT-

IF YOU ARE IN A GROUP ATMOSPHERE, DO NOT PICK UP A BOOK AND READ WHILE YOU'RE AT THE INTERVIEW!

MINGLE, MINGLE, MINGLE!

Someone is always watching. Mingle and get to know people. Airlines want to see that you can be friendly and talk to anyone you cross paths with. Smile!

WHAT MAKES A GOOD FLIGHT ATTENDANT?

You might be asked to stand up in front of the room to introduce yourself and give a brief description of what you think makes a good flight attendant. Here is a list of strong adjectives that describe what it means to be a good flight attendant, HOWEVER, don't just stand there and list off a handful of these words. Work these words into your description. *This is your time to shine.* Treat it like an acting audition. Be expressive! Smile big! Look around the room and into the eyes of the other candidates and at the interviewers standing at the back of the room. Believe me, they are always taking notes. Candidates will blend in, so say something memorable. Be unique.

STRONG DESCRIPTIVE WORDS

Circle or highlight the words that you like best or that describe you.

- Adaptive
- Adventurous
- Alert
- Ambitious
- Attentive
- Calm
- Calming
- Capable
- Caring
- Charming
- Confident
- Considerate
- Courteous
- Creative
- Credible
- Customer Service Oriented
- Dedicated
- Delightful
- Dependable
- Diligent
- Diplomatic
- Discrete
- Discerning
- Dynamic
- Eager
- Easy Going
- Efficient
- Encouraging
- Energetic
- Enthusiastic
- Fashionable
- Friendly
- Fun
- Funny
- Graceful
- Genuine
- Helpful
- Honorable
- Honest
- Innovative
- Instinctive
- Listens Carefully
- Observant
- Organized
- Outgoing
- Passionate
- Plans Ahead
- Punctual
- Reassuring
- Resourceful
- Sensitive to Others
- Sophisticated
- Supporter
- Takes Initiative
- Team Leader
- Team Player
- Thoughtful
- Trustworthy

INTERVIEW QUESTIONS

Here are examples of the types of questions that may be asked in a flight attendant interview. Always try to put a positive spin on your answer even when answering the difficult or hard to answer ones.

Answer these questions now so you can be prepared for the real interview:

1. Tell me about yourself. *(Do you find it so difficult to brag about yourself in an interview? Write out some things about who you are so you have something to share at the front of your mind.)*

_____
_____

2. Why do you want to be a flight attendant? *(PLEASE Think of an answer other than "I want to travel and I like people." That's the standard answer. Come up with something more original.)*

_____
_____

3. Think about a time when you had a difficult time working with a co-worker. What did you do? How did you resolve the conflict?

_____
_____

4. What is your greatest strength?

_____
_____

5. What is your greatest weakness? *(Remember to put a positive spin on this. Everyone has a weakness. Don't say you don't have one.)*

_____
_____

6. Why do you want to work for this airline over all the other airlines?
(Remember all the things you researched about the company.)
_____
_____

7. Why would you be a good fit to be a flight attendant?
_____
_____

8. Have you ever had a problem with a customer and how did you resolve it?
_____
_____

9. If you were the lead flight attendant and a co-worker on your crew was not doing their job, what would you do?
_____
_____

10. Give an example of a time you went out of your way for a customer.
_____
_____

11. What is your greatest achievement in your life so far?
_____
_____

12. Name a misconception people have about you.
_____
_____

13. What does diversity mean to you and what does it look like in the workplace?
_____
_____

14. How would you handle an unruly passenger?
_____
_____

15. Why are you interested in leaving your current employer?
_____
_____

16. How do you react to confrontation?
_____
_____

17. What do you think will be the most challenging aspect about being a flight attendant?
_____
_____

18. What kind of things anger or frustrate you? *(Speak calmly about this topic.)*
_____
_____

19. How do you handle stress? *(Working on an airplane in tight quarters may be stressful and there's nowhere to retreat.)*
_____
_____

20. Describe the way you work when under pressure or a tight deadline.
_____
_____

21. Tell me about a time that you received excellent customer service.
_____
_____
_____

PHYSICAL REQUIREMENTS

WEIGHT REQUIREMENTS
In the United States, a company cannot require you to be a certain weight.

THE JUMPSEAT TEST
Every time a flight attendant works a flight, he or she must be seated in their jumpseat next to their assigned emergency exit door during takeoff and landing. If you fit, you've passed the test.

HEIGHT TEST
In the "Job Requirements" section of the application, a company might specify that applicants need to be within a certain height range, but no one will be getting out their ruler to see if you are within the specified height. There will be an area with a section of an airplane fuselage set up complete with overhead bins. Take off your shoes and reach into the overhead bin to retrieve an object and then put it back again. This is how the airlines determine if you are tall enough for the job.

HISTORY LESSON
Back in the olden days, flight attendants had to be a certain height and weight and would be periodically checked to see if they were maintaining their appearances.

That was SO 1962....

CONGRATULATIONS, YOU GOT THE JOB!

THE JOB OFFER!

There are two ways in which the company will offer you the job.

-Send you home and contact you later offering you the job

OR

-The most exhilarating way: they might offer you the job…

RIGHT THERE ON THE SPOT!

-WARNING-

Tears of absolute joy may begin to fill your eyes and stream down your face. Childlike screaming and shrieking may overcome you.

WELCOME TO THE FAMILY OF AVIATION!

Big hugs are allowed and encouraged upon finding out you got the job! Be prepared to fill out a giant stack of paperwork, have your fingerprints taken, and have a photo taken for your employee badge. Hope you're having a great hair day because that photo they take of you will be on your badge FOR-EV-ER.

THE PHONE CALL

Alright, so now it's time to call your family and friends and share with them the good news. It may be hard to contain yourself. Try not to blow out your loved one's eardrums because you are screaming with excitement. Now it's time to fly or drive home! If you are flying home, I suggest you bring a change of clothes. You've been dressed to impress all day and now it's time to relax. Still keep it respectable, but bring something you are more comfortable in and change once you get back to the airport.

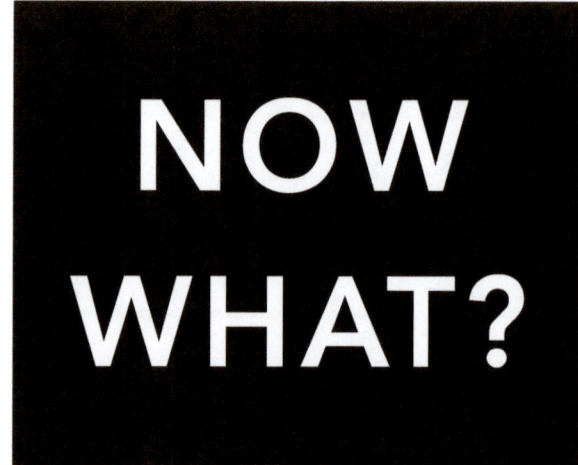

SAVE, SAVE, SAVE!

Start a savings account, if you don't already have one. Between now and the time you start training, you will want to put aside as much money as you possibly can. Any money you have saved up is what will get you through training and possibly even until your first paycheck which could be two to four weeks after you first start flying. Training could be 4-8 weeks, so budget accordingly.

ACCOMODATIONS

Most likely, your airline will pay for your accommodations while you are in training. They may put you up in a hotel or dormitory housing at the training facility. Whether you are in a hotel or in dorm housing, there may be a chance that you have a roommate for the duration of your training. Check with your airline.

POSSIBLE EXPENSES

Often times, airlines will not pay you while you are in training. If your airline does pay you for training, or if they give you a signing bonus, then you've picked well. Check to see if any meals will be included, whether that's at the training facility or at the hotel or location of accommodation. Plan on a majority of the airlines not to pay you during training. You will need to save money for these possible expenses:

Food - Transportation - Clothing - Dry Cleaning

Personal Products - Laundry Detergent

Make a list of any additional items that you will need to set money aside for while you are away at training. This may include expenses back at home as well.

_____   _____

_____   _____

_____   _____

_____   _____

READY FOR TRAINING?

SERIOUSLY, HOW HARD IS IT TO POUR A DIET COKE?

Okay, well hopefully there isn't any blood, but you can guarantee there will be lots of sweat and a few tears here and there. Don't get me wrong, this is going to be an amazing time. You're going to make some lifelong friends in training and this is going to be one of the best experiences of your life. It's also going to be one of the toughest things you've ever done. Mentally prepare yourself for training. It can be very draining and even boring at times with really long days up to six days a week. Think about taking 12 college credits over the course of a semester and cramming all that course work and information into your brain over the course of a few weeks. Yup, you got the picture.

Someone might ask, "What can possibly take you a month to learn? I thought flight attendants just served drinks?" Well, let me tell you! It is most likely that you will learn about serving food and drinks on the airplane for a maximum of two to three days. The rest of the time will be about learning to evacuate the airplane in a matter of minutes, preparing the airplane for emergency landings or water ditchings, taking care of unusual scenarios, and spotting suspicious behavior. Bring a good set of lungs and your shouting voice, because you'll need them to practice emergency evacuation commands to passengers. You will repeat these commands until you are blue in the face and need oxygen yourself! You will be able to say these commands in your sleep by the end of training.

You'll be jumping through airplane windows and down evacuation slides. It's going to be an intense time, but you'll look back at it as one of the best experiences of your life.

You will learn so much about yourself and find you are more capable than you ever thought possible.

As far as the Diet Coke goes, you'll learn to cringe every time someone asks for one on the airplane. There is something about being at 30,000 feet and the artificial sweetener makes it fizz like crazy and it takes forever to go away. You can pour three other cups of soda in the time it takes for the fizz in a quarter of a glass of Diet Coke to go away so you can finish pouring the drink.

DOWN TIME
After being in class for nearly ten hours a day, I had only enough energy to grab a bite to eat from the hotel lobby, run upstairs to change, and then sit in the hot tub with two or three friends for about twenty minutes before retiring to my room for the rest of the night to study. Even though life will be crazy for 4-8 weeks, be sure to make time for some "me" time, even if it's just twenty minutes a day.

PHYSICAL HEALTH
Stay hydrated!!! It can be very easy to get dehydrated. Drink as much water as you can throughout the day. I would suggest buying a nice water bottle and keeping it with you throughout the day. You might want the caffeine but I would suggest staying away from the coffee because it makes dehydration worse. One of my closest friends during training got dehydrated to the point where she almost passed out and the paramedics were called. She was so light headed she could hardly sit up straight in her chair.

EATING WELL
Your brain needs the food you eat just as much as your stomach does. Be sure to eat enough during the day and while you are studying.

WORKING OUT
If you are a very active person like myself and you love to workout, don't hold too high of an expectation for your workouts to stay consistent. Don't be hard on yourself, but do what you can to keep active. Honestly, some days sleeping will be the most important part of the day. You will have nights where you feel like you just fell asleep and then the alarm is buzzing a few minutes later.

DRESSING FOR TRAINING

You will be required to wear professional business attire each day at training or your uniforms. Uniforms may be ordered at the time of training or beforehand and you must bring them with you. I suggest bringing a sweater or a jacket to the classroom because most times they will have the air pumping through the building and rooms are often on the cooler side.

Bring casual clothes as well. On the days where you will be jumping down the evacuation slide and practicing the use of putting out real fires with fire extinguishers, you will be asked to wear casual clothes.

Bring a set of clothes you don't mind getting wet. There will be a day when everyone has to jump into a pool and swim out to a life raft. If you wear a swimsuit, wear a t-shirt and shorts over it as well. Can't swim? Your fellow classmates will be there to guide you safely to the raft.

AIRPORT CODES

Airport Codes are going to be your new best friend. One thing about airlines, there is often so much information to communicate on a daily basis that they have it down to an abbreviated science. Every single airport in the world has an identifier code. It doesn't matter if the airport is super small and can only handle small single engine airplanes or is the biggest airport in the world - all airports have a three character code. Most of the big airports only use letters.

Some are no brainers like DEN is the code for Denver. Then they can get super confusing like ORD for Chicago. This one makes you think "Who on earth came up with those letters to represent Chicago?!?" These less than obvious codes often derive from something other than the name of the city, most likely the name of the airport, or the for the region surrounding the airport. ORD stands for the Orchard Field. Get an official list from your airline as to which cities they fly into and the codes that you will need to memorize. On page 85 you can find all the major airport codes.

> **MANY AIRLINES WILL TEST YOU ON ALL THE AIRPORT CODES ON YOUR FIRST DAY OF TRAINING! STUDY UP AND GET TO KNOW THEM NOW!**

DIDN'T LAND THE JOB? DON'T GIVE UP. TRY, TRY AGAIN.

If you made it all the way to the in-person interview and didn't get the job, you now know how the process goes for that airline and what they are looking for. Keep doing your research on that and other airlines. Some airlines may only hire a certain number of people out of each interview group. It may have been a matter of too many people hired that day. That might sound ridiculous, but sometimes it's true. Again, don't give up, and keep applying.

AIRPORT CODES

ABE Allentown, PA
ACA Acapulco, Mexico
ALB Albany, NY
AMA Amarillo, TX
AMS Amsterdam, Netherlands
ANC Anchorage, AK
ASP Aspen, CO
ATL Atlanta, GA
ACY Atlantic City, NJ
AKL Auckland, New Zealand
AUS Austin, TX
BAI Buenos Aires, Costa Rica
BDL Hartford, CT
BAQ Barranquilla, Columbia
BCN Barcelona, Spain
BGR Bangor, Maine
BGY Milan, Italy
BHM Birmingham, AL
BHX Birmingham, England
BKK Bangkok, Thailand
BKA Moscow, Russia
BJS Beijing, China
BMA Stockholm, Sweden
BNA Nashville, TN
BOG Bogata, Columbia
BOI Boise, ID
BOM Bombay, India
BOS Boston, MA
BPT Beaumont, TX
BRU Brussels, Belgium
BUD Budapest, Hungary
BUE Buenos Aires, Argentina
BUF Buffalo, NY

CAI Cairo, Egypt
CAK Canton/Akron, OH
CDG Paris, France Charles De Gaulle
CLE Cleveland, OH
CLT Charlotte, NC
COS Colorado Springs, CO
CRP Corpus Christie, TX
CZM Cozumel, Mexico
CVG Cincinnati, OH
DAB Daytona Beach, FL
DFW Dallas/Fort Worth, TX
DAL Dallas Love Field, TX
DAY Daytona, OH
DCA Washington, DC
DEN Denver, CO
DSM Des Moines, IA
DUB Dublin, Ireland
DTW Detroit, MI
EWR Newark, NJ
ELP El Paso, TX
FAI Fairbanks, AK
FAT Fresno, CA
FCO Rome, Italy
FLL Fort Lauderdale, FL
FLR Florence, Italy
FRA Frankfurt, Germany
GIG Rio De Janeiro, Brazil
HKG Hong Kong
HTS Huntington, WV
HNL Honolulu, HI
GVA Geneva, Switzerland
GRB Green Bay, WI
GRR Grand Rapids, MI

GLA	Glasgow, Scotland
GCM	Grand Cayman, West Indies
GDL	Guadalajara, Mexico
GSO	Greensboro, NC
GSP	Greenville/Spartenburg, SC
JFK	New York, NY John F Kennedy
JAN	Jackson, MS
JAX	Jacksonville, FL
IND	Indianapolis, IN
IST	Istanbul, Turkey
ITO	Hilo, HI
IAD	Washington, Dulles
IAH	Houston, TX
ICT	Wichita, KS
HOU	Houston, TX Hobby Airport
KOA	Kona, HI
LAS	Las Vegas, NV
LIH	Lihue, HI
LIS	Lisbon, Portugal
LYS	Lyon, France
LUX	Luxembourg
LEX	Lexington, KY
LIT	Little Rock, AR
LGA	New York, NY La Guardia Airport
LGB	Long Beach, CA
LGW	London, England Gatwick
LHR	London, England Heathrow
MEM	Memphis, TN
MCO	Orlando, FL
MAD	Madrid, Spain
MAN	Manchester, England
MBJ	Montego Bay, Jamaica
MDW	Chicago, IL Midway Airport
MEX	Mexico City, Mexico
MIA	Miami, FL
MKE	Milwaukee, WI
MSY	New Orleans, LA
MSP	Minneapolis/ St. Paul, MN
MUC	Munich, Germany
MYR	Myrtle Beach, SC
MTY	Monterey, Mexico
NAP	Naples, Italy
NAS	Nassau, Bahamas
NRT	Tokyo, Japan
OAK	Oakland, CA
OGG	Maui, HI
ORD	Chicago, IL O'Hare Airport
ORY	Paris, France Orly Airport
PBI	Palm Beach, FL
PDX	Portland, OR
PER	Perth, Australia
PHL	Philadelphia, PA
PIT	Pittsburgh, Pa
PHX	Phoenix, AZ
PSP	Palm Springs, CA
PVD	Providence, RI
PWM	Portland, M
RDU	Raleigh/Durham, NC
SAN	San Diego, CA
SAT	San Antonio, TX
SCL	Santiago, Chili
SDF	Louisville, KY
SEA	Seattle, WA
SFO	San Francisco, CA
SJC	San Jose, CA
SLC	Salt Lake City, UT
SMF	Sacramento, CA
SYD	Sydney, Australia
YYC	Calgary, Alberta, Canada
YUL	Montreal, Canada
YOW	Ottawa
YHZ	Halifax, Canada
YVR	Vancouver, Canada

24-HOUR CLOCK

Instead of having to specify time in AM and PM, airlines operate on military time or the 24-hour clock. If you are not familiar with the 24-hour clock, I suggest learning that now.

Here is the conversion:

12:00am : 0000	12:00pm : 1200
1:00am : 0100	1:00pm : 1300
2:00am : 0200	2:00pm : 1400
3:00am : 0300	3:00pm : 1500
4:00am : 0400	4:00pm : 1600
5:00am : 0500	5:00pm : 1700
6:00am : 0600	6:00pm : 1800
7:00am : 0700	7:00pm : 1900
8:00am : 0800	8:00pm : 2000
9:00am : 0900	9:00pm : 2100
10:00am : 1000	10:00pm : 2200
11:00am : 1100	11:00pm : 2300

-WARNING-

Be sure not to confuse the times. It's easy to confuse 1600 for 6:00pm.

When trying to figure out the 24-hour clock, subtract 1200 from the time and you'll get the normal time.

Example: 2256
          -1200
           1056 = 10:56pm

KEY TERMS

- **Airport Codes:** Three-letter code used to represent the name of the airport.
- **Air Traffic Control (ATC):** A ground-based service that directs airplane traffic at airports and in flight.
- **Altitude:** The height above the ground the airplane is flying.
- **Base:** A city or airport which an airline runs daily operations out of.
- **Badge or ID:** Picture identification that must be worn or carried at all times.
- **Beverage Cart:** Large metal cart narrow enough to fit down airplane aisles that holds beverages, ice, and snacks.
- **Bidding:** The process in which flight attendants pick out their desired schedules in preferred order.
- **Bid Sheet:** A packet with trips and flight schedules that flight attendants pick from to bid for their schedules.
- **Block Holder:** A flight attendant who bids for a set schedule of flights each month.
- **Block Schedule:** Often referred to as a "block" - the monthly schedule that block holders bid for.
- **Catering:** A department in the airline that brings food, beverages, and supplies on board the airplane.
- **Check-in:** The time you must report and check in at the airport. Generally an hour before the flight departs.
- **Check Ride:** A supervisor rides as a passenger on your flight during your probation period and observes your duties, taking notes on performance, and evaluating whether you are doing your job correctly or not.
- **Cockpit:** The area at the front of the airplane where the pilots sit and control the airplane.
- **Commercial Airline:** An airline that offers flights to the general public.
- **Commuter:** A crew member who lives in one city and takes an airplane to the city in which they work usually flying stand-by. This makes for a very long day.
- **Contract:** Flight attendants have contracts with the airline that states the terms and conditions for pay, work environments, and accommodations.
- **Corporate Airline:** A company that is privately owned and operated that only offers flights to owners or share-owners.
- **Crew Member:** Any flight attendants or pilots.

- **Crew Scheduling:** The scheduling service that calls flight attendants to assign trips.
- **Daily Scheduling:** Scheduling that manages and assigns you a trip for that day.
- **Deadhead:** Crew member traveling as a passenger in uniform on company business.
- **Domestic:** Any flight that stays within the country. Alaska and Hawaii may or may not be considered domestic due to the distance away. Check with your airline.
- **Ditching:** Having to do an emergency evacuation after the airplane has landed in water.
- **Divert:** Having to fly to a different airport other than the original destination due to weather, emergency, or other situation.
- **Duty Free:** Items bought on the airplane that are tax free.
- **Emergency Equipment:** Required equipment on each airplane in case of an emergency usually consisting of items such as life vests, portable oxygen, etc.
- **Emergency Exit:** Door or window on the airplane intended for use in an emergency evacuation.
- **Evacuation:** Rapidly leaving the airplane due to an emergency through available doors and evacuation windows.
- **Evacuation Slide:** Slide that deploys from emergency doors and windows that allow passengers to slide them to the ground in the case of an emergency.
- **Federal Air Marshal (FAM):** A law enforcement officer who travels undercover in civilian clothes to offer protection on flights.
- **Federal Aviation Administration (FAA):** Governing agency that is the national authority on aviation.
- **Ferry Flight:** A flight without passengers, but the airplane must be transported to another location. A full crew is generally required for this flight.
- **First Officer:** The pilot in the right seat of the cockpit, has 3 stripes on the shoulder, and is second in command. Knows how to fly just as well as the captain.
- **Flight Time:** The actual time in flight from wheels up to landing.
- **Future Scheduling:** Scheduling that manages and assigns all trips for the following day.
- **Galley:** A small kitchenette area in the front, middle, or back of the airplane.
- **Jet Bridge:** The mechanical hallway stretching out from the terminal of the airport to the door of the airplane.
- **Jumpseat (noun):** A fold-out seat along the wall of the airplane reserved for flight attendants only. Certain jumpseats are required to have flight attendants seated in them during take-off and landing.
- **Lavatory (Lav):** Fancy name for the bathroom on the airplane.
- **Layover:** The time spent in a city, generally overnight, while not on the airplane.

- **Lead or "Purser" Flight Attendant**: Head flight attendant on the trip who designates duties and is the main communicator with the flight crew and gate agents.
- **Leg:** A single flight from one city to the next. You can have upwards of 3-5 legs a day.
- **Mainline:** A major airline that offers long flights in larger aircraft and operates under its own name unlike a regional airline.
- **Manual:** A set of rules, regulations, and standards physically printed in a book or on an electronic resource such as a tablet. Manuals are required by the FAA to be on hand or close by during every flight.
- **On-Premise Reserve:** A flight attendant who is working an on-call shift while sitting at the airport in case a trip needs to be covered within minutes. On-premise reserve shifts may be 3-5 hours long.
- **Non-Revenue Passengers (Non-Revs):** A passenger flying for free or at a discounted rate flying stand-by or waiting for an empty seat.
- **Per Diem:** An amount the company will pay you per hour for time away from home while not on the airplane. Usually designated for cost of food.
- **Regional:** Regional airlines offer shorter flights on smaller aircrafts. Regional airlines often fly under a major name such as American or United but are operated by a separate company.
- **Recurrent Training:** Annual training that a crew member must attend to stay current with all the aircraft they are qualified on and any safety, evacuation drills, or first aid training.
- **Remain On-Call (ROC):** If scheduling calls you to assign you a trip that you are not eligible to work, they will have you remain on call.
- **Reserve Flight Attendant:** A flight attendant who is "on-call" or who is being held "on reserve" to fill in when the airline needs you.
- **Revolving Reserve:** Some companies offer a revolving reserve system so that people don't have to remain on reserve for years on end, but rather have a rotation between reserve months and months holding a block.
- **Quick Call:** When scheduling assigns a trip that requires a check-in within a minimal amount of time. Usually 90 minutes to 2 hours depending on the amount designated by the flight attendant contract.
- **Safety Demo:** A demonstration on the airplane to all the passengers about the safety equipment, seat belt operations, and location of exits and flotation devices.
- **Steward/Stewardess**: For those who are too young to remember, a steward or stewardess was the original name for flight attendant.
- **Stand-by:** Waiting at the airport with your name on a wait-list for an open seat on the airplane.

- **Slam-clicker:** A crew member who gets to their hotel room, slams the door shut, clicks the lock, and doesn't come out until it's time to catch the van back to the airport.
- **Senior Mamma:** A flight attendant who has been working a long time at the company, generally with 25-40 years of experience and seniority.
- **Taxi:** When the airplane is in motion on the ground.
- **Unaccompanied Minor:** A child under the age of 18 traveling by themselves. The child will be escorted by a guardian through security to the gate agent where they sign for the child, then the child is transferred to the flight attendant for the flight. Once the final destination is reached, the flight attendant will sign the child over to the gate agent who then accompanies the child to the guardian waiting for them at the gate.
- **Union:** The body of workers who have come together to represent the individual workers and protect against unfair labor, wage protection, and safety issues. The union negotiates with the airline on behalf of its members.
- **Wheels Up Time:** This is the projected time the airplane is scheduled to be airborne.

NOTES

NOTES

THANK YOU!

Mom, Dad, and Christopher,
Thank you for supporting me as I figure out how to spread my wings and fly both figuratively and literally. Your unconditional love has helped me achieve far more than I could have ever imagined.

Eric,
All I expected to do was take flying lessons, but you have become my best friend, my heart, my husband and my travel buddy. Thank you for teaching me to fly. Every day you teach me more about living a life I can be proud of.

Jenae,
Thank you for pushing me to break away from my norm and chase after my dreams. You believed in me even when I wasn't sure of myself yet.

Editors: Jenae Hull, Pat Urban, and Barb Smith.